Crying
for the Light

Crying
for the Light

Bible Readings and Reflections for Living with Depression

Veronica Zundel

Kregel *Publications*

U.S. edition © 2009 Kregel Publications, Grand Rapids, Michigan, published by special arrangement with The Bible Reading Fellowship, 15 The Chambers, Vineyard, Abingdon OX14 3FE, www.brf.org.uk.

ISBN 978-0-8254-4165-3

Printed in the United States of America

09 10 11 12 13 / 5 4 3 2 1

Contents

Contents

Foreword

This book is a gem, giving helpful, factual information about depression while engaging the reader at many different levels. There are prayers and poems that speak directly to anyone in mental distress while the Bible readings are pithy and enlightening. Veronica tells the fascinating story of her struggles with life and love, and the final section of the book is a searingly honest exploration of depression and faith that helpfully deconstructs some of the spiritual nonsense we can be told.

This is a book full of insight and sensitive, intelligent observations about life. It is divided into small, bite-sized pieces, just right when one's attention span seems to be about ten seconds. It is something to keep by your bedside to dip into when you want spiritual and emotional direction in those moments of despair.

Veronica has written a book of great integrity about real issues that face real people who don't want to be fobbed off with glib statements. *Crying for the Light* is a book of hope because it tells it how it is.

People often ask me what they can do to help a depressed person. It's been hard to give a helpful answer to that, but from now on I will suggest that they buy a copy of Veronica's book.

SUE ATKINSON

Introduction

This is a book about depression and other forms of emotional distress or mental illness. Why another book on this topic? And can books help anyway? Those are fair questions. Reading may be our only escape from depression, or it can seem like just one more burden when our concentration is shot to pieces by our illness or the medication we take for it.

I suppose I am writing this because I am mostly in the first category: I love to read something—fiction or nonfiction—that tells me that someone else has been through what I have been through. My poem "Put a Name" (which you will find in my story on page 70) was inspired by reading a novel, written in the late nineteenth century, whose heroine was suffering from unrequited and hopeless love. For me, that experience was significant because I had read any number of novels portraying this pain from a male viewpoint, but this was the first I had read that portrayed it so accurately from a young female viewpoint. Since unrequited love is one of my great hobbies, I felt recognized and affirmed.

I have suffered from depression for nearly thirty-five years and have been medicated for it intermittently for the last thirty and constantly for the past fifteen. I am also a writer. Writing is one of the things I enjoy most in life, and it seemed logical to bring together my writing and my experience of depression and breakdown. One of my main writing jobs is writing comments on the Bible, helping people to find reflections of and on their own lives in its words. So it also seemed logical for part of this book to consist of reflections on the Bible, along with prayers, poems, and liturgy inspired both by life and by the Bible.

Introduction

This is not a self-help book, a medical textbook, or a complete guide to the alien land of depression or mental illness. There are plenty of books like those already. It is more of an attempt to tell one Christian's story, to hear the voices of others with similar experiences, and to discover whether the Bible can both echo our experience and play a part in healing our wounds.

What It's All About

In this introduction I want to give a brief outline of depression and related illnesses and explain the structure of this book.

The first thing to say—and it can never be repeated too often—is that depression is an illness. So are bipolar disorder, psychosis, schizophrenia, personality disorder, generalized anxiety disorder, obsessive-compulsive disorder, or anything else with which the readers (and writer) of this book may be diagnosed. These illnesses are not demon possession, they are not signs of a lack of faith, and they generally are not going to be healed by more prayer, or by pronouncing them the work of the Devil or accusing their sufferers of being more sinful than others.

Most sensible Christians, if presented with someone who has cancer, a broken leg, or a chest infection, will tell the sufferer to go to the doctor. They may also pray or advise the other person to pray, but they will not prescribe prayer as an alternative to medical help. Why should it be any different with illnesses of the mind?

Depression is an illness of the mind and emotions. So are all the other illnesses I have listed above. Some are more easily treated than others but all can be medically identified and medically alleviated, if not cured.

I'm not going to say a lot about mental illness in general, because I'm not qualified to do so, and there are other places where you can get this information (some are listed in the Resources section at the end of the book). My late brother, who died at his own hand in the

1970s, had a mental illness that was never adequately diagnosed, although I suspect it might nowadays be called generalized anxiety disorder—but that is the only other mental health problem with which I have direct experience. Depression is the only one I have experienced from the inside, so I will say a little about that.

Depression is of two kinds: reactive (caused by an identifiable external event or situation) and endogenous (having no obvious outside cause). It is characterized by symptoms such as:

- general lowness of mood
- numbness, lack of enjoyment
- anxiety
- irritability
- uncontrollable weeping or inability to cry
- inability to do tasks that are usually easy
- difficulty being in others' company or in being alone
- inability to concentrate
- panic attacks
- difficulty sleeping, or difficulty staying awake
- loss of appetite, or "comfort eating"
- loss of sexual feelings
- an overwhelmingly negative view of life or one's own life

A sufferer may have all of these symptoms or only one or two. There can also be physical symptoms like nausea, stomachache, "butterflies," facial twitches, muscle tension, and hand tremors.

Depression can be mild or severe; it can be accompanied by frightening symptoms such as dissociation (going off into a "world of one's own," impervious to external stimuli), sudden mood swings, irrational fears, self-harm, intrusive thoughts, violent compulsions toward oneself or others, or suicidal feelings. It can also be a cause, or a by-product, of alcohol abuse, drug abuse, or eating disorders.

Some people think that depression is caused by chemical changes in the brain, some that those chemical changes are a result of depression. Either way, depression generally goes together with chemical or hormonal changes in the brain, which means that taking medications that alter brain chemistry can relieve or even cure it.

Things That Help

Treatment for depression, as for other psychiatric illnesses, can take various forms. Antidepressants or other medications prescribed by a doctor (such as antipsychotics or lithium for mood swings) can transform some people's lives. There should be no more shame in taking these medicines than there is in taking antibiotics for an infection or insulin for diabetes. A family doctor or a psychiatrist, according to the severity and length of the illness, may prescribe medication.

Sometimes, medication just gets us to the point of being ready to try one of the bewildering array of "talk therapies." Counseling, or psychotherapy, comes in a huge variety of forms. Some are based on talk alone, while others include work on how we relate to and use our bodies; the therapeutic use of art or music; work in groups; or ways of "dramatizing" our situation—such as Gestalt therapy, in which we talk to a chair representing significant people in our life. (The Resources section includes ways of finding out about different therapies.)

The terms "counseling" and "psychotherapy" are sometimes used interchangeably, which can be confusing. I prefer to use the term "counselor" for those who have had some training in understanding people in general, well or ill, and who provide a safe space for us to consider our life and choices and perhaps give us some advice. "Psychotherapist" is a term I would rather reserve for those who have had considerable training in one or more of the classic or more modern forms of therapy used to treat people who have been diagnosed by a doctor as clinically depressed or mentally ill.

I generally advise people to see a doctor first, since it is important to look for possible medical conditions that can be related to depression. If you have medical insurance, a referral from your family doctor may be required in order to see a psychiatrist or licensed psychologist. Many communities have mental health service centers that include a range of services from psychiatrists, psychologists, or licensed counselors. No referral may be required for their services. Some communities may also have counseling centers organized by Christian agencies that offer counseling from a Christian perspective.

In recent years, a lot of publicity has been given to CBT, or cognitive behavior therapy (sometimes called emotional or rational-emotional behavior therapy). This is therapy focused on the patient's habits of thinking and acting, given in a short course of sessions, resulting in changes of habit and action. It has been known to get significant results in a short time.

I want to emphasize again and again, at the risk of being boring, that no one need be ashamed of seeking help through the medical profession or through psychotherapy. People often are, sadly, because they think others will think them crazy or stupid. "Mental illness" carries a social stigma that does not come with, say, going to the dentist with an impacted wisdom tooth. The only way to overcome that stigma, however, is for us "crazies" to come out of our corner and be unashamed about our needs. Anyone ready to join me here on this platform? No? Take as long as you need.

A Virtual Lifeboat

There are, of course, many things you can do to promote your own emotional healing and to supplement any professional help you get. They include good diet, sleeping at regular times, regular exercise, giving yourself little treats (which needn't cost much), reading books or watching TV programs that take you out of yourself, listening to music you love, getting a massage, spending time with friends, going to a church that supports rather than demoralizes you, avoiding situations that you know are going to be too much, saying no to demands you can't meet, and many other activities that I need to remind myself of, just as much as you do! Often we unconsciously sabotage our health by failing to do these things, and we need to learn that we deserve self-care as much as anyone else.

For mild to moderate depression, over-the-counter herbal remedies such as St. John's wort, valerian, or herbal sleeping tablets can be helpful—but do remember that these are all chemical substances, and you should check with your doctor about their compatibility with any other medication you may be taking (including medications for physical symptoms). Moreover, they don't agree with everyone and, like all medications, can have side effects.

One course of action I definitely do not recommend is trying to self-medicate with alcohol or "street drugs." The former is a depressant, the latter are illegal and often dangerous, and all are potentially addictive. If you are reading this and have a problem with alcohol or drugs, you can get help from your local branch of Alcoholics Anonymous or a local drug treatment service, as soon as you recognize that you have a problem.

Something I've discovered more recently is the support that people "in the same boat" can give each other. Over the past few years, I have belonged to the Internet forum run by Ship of Fools: the Webzine of Christian unrest (www.ship-of-fools.com). Ship of Fools has a large and thriving number of bulletin boards, including one that exists just to bring "shipmates" together through common experiences, or in real-life "shipmeets."

One day I plucked up the courage to ask if anyone else on the

Introduction

Ship suffered from depression. I was overwhelmed with responses, and many said that they would feel more free to discuss their illness if they could do so on a private board, which could be set up under the umbrella of the Ship for a small fee. I recklessly volunteered to start it, and the result was Waving, Not Drowning, a growing online community of over a hundred people who support, inform, and challenge each other, as well as pray for each other and sometimes meet face to face. I am the founding "host" but, as I write, there are three others whom I have invited to manage and protect this vulnerable group of people. None of us are experts except in our own condition, but we are there to give encouragement, help, and occasionally friendly advice to each other. I've been amazed how supportive a "virtual community" can be. (Sometimes we even send each other real chocolate!)

Early in the board's life, one member suggested that since there were few understanding prayers about mental health issues, we should write our own. The outcome was a collection of honest, insightful prayers and liturgy, and I have included a selection scattered among the Bible readings in this book. Some of the writers have chosen to be identified by their real names, some by pseudonyms, and some by initials.

I have also included a few of my own poems and some written by poets far more famous than I am. Later in the book, you will find my own story of life with depression, some reflections on faith and depression and, finally, the Resources section.

This, then, is a "book of bits," as Spike Milligan put it (who himself suffered from mental illness). You can dip into it as you feel able, taking what helps and leaving the rest. I hope it will be a way of feeling less alone in your situation; maybe even people who aren't suffering mental health problems will read it to understand their friends or relatives better.

The title *Crying for the Light* comes from Tennyson's long poem

"In Memoriam AHH" (1850), grieving the death of a close friend. Here are the relevant verses.

> Behold; we know not anything;
> I can but trust that good shall fall
> At last—far off—at last, to all,
> And every winter change to spring.
> So runs my dream: but what am I?
> An infant crying in the night:
> An infant crying for the light:
> And with no language but a cry.

If that seems like a cry of despair, consider this: those of us who are followers of Jesus believe that the light exists even when we cannot see it; that there are fatherly, motherly arms which will one day embrace the infants we are, and show that they have understood the language of our cry from the beginning.

Songs in the Darkness: Readings from the Psalms

"Like vinegar on a wound is one who sings songs to a heavy heart," says the writer of Proverbs (25:20). In the midst of depression, you may well have the same reaction to someone who advises you to read the Bible.

Maybe the Bible has been presented to you as a book of rules, of exhortations to do the right thing—not easy to take when you haven't got the energy to get out of bed. Or maybe you have overdosed on Scripture-based songs of praise, and you feel more like cursing than praising God.

When I was suffering a severe depression, with violent and terrifying compulsions, the most I could manage was to repeat Psalm 23 to myself from memory. Someone else's "blessed thoughts" would have driven me even deeper into darkness and helplessness.

So why a series of Bible readings on depression? Because the Bible is not just a book of "Thou shalt" and "Thou shalt not" but, among other things, a record of all kinds of human experience, including the most painful emotions a human being can suffer. Perhaps the most revealing, honest, and accessible biblical picture of emotional pain is the book of poems we call the Psalms—so here are my thoughts on some of what I call "the depressive Psalms."

Grief, sadness, guilt, envy, and anger are emotions that we may hesitate to reveal. The psalmists came from a more expressive culture, and we will find passionate language in these worship poems. That is why I have used Eugene H. Peterson's daring paraphrase *The Message* (with my own paraphrases on Days 1 and 4). You may love or hate it: if the latter, feel free to look up a more traditional version.

I have written my comment as a diary, to get inside the experience of emotional pain. Depression does not follow a straightforward course from illness to health, so rather than trying to fit the readings into some sort of progression, I have simply followed the biblical order of the Psalms. You will find that one day is more upbeat, and then it's followed by another "down"—just as depression behaves in real life.

You don't need to follow these readings every day. You might want to select just one element from the mix of reading, comment, and prayer exercises. You might read them in a different order, or skip any that seem too sad or too cheerful. However you use them, I hope that you will be able to recognize your own pain reflected in the Bible, and to recognize God at the heart of the pain.

Day 1

Down and Out

Focus: To focus your thoughts, sit comfortably and breathe deeply for a few moments. Repeat the word "God" in time with your breathing. Accept any emotions that surface as a result. Then read the paraphrase of Psalm 6 below.

> God, do you have to keep telling me off?
> What are you punishing me for?
> Please, oh please, be kinder to me,
> I'm so weak and faint;
> make it better, Lord—I can't stop shaking.
> It feels like my bones are all broken
> and my soul's a limp rag, terrified.
> How long does this have to go on?
> I don't think I've ever been so exhausted.
> I soak my bed with tears every night;
> my eyes are so swollen
> I can hardly see at all
> because of this deep, deep sadness.
>
> BASED ON PSALM 6:1–3, 6–7

"Nobody told me that grief would feel so like fear," wrote C. S. Lewis in *A Grief Observed*. How I understand—the trembling, the tightening of the stomach, the paralysis, like a nightmare in which you can't run away from your pursuer. Is it sadness at the past? Is it terror of the present? It makes little difference—even if it's a reaction to a long-ago pain, I still feel as bad as if it were happening now. Crying helps but I hate to do it in front of strangers, and sometimes I can't stop, and I end up swollen-eyed, exhausted. How long can I bear this?

I must have done something wrong, made God angry somehow. Has God lost patience with me? What is it Julian of Norwich says? "I saw no wrath in God, but only in man." Perhaps it's my own anger I feel. That phrase from Nehemiah keeps going round my mind: "A God . . . slow to anger and abounding in steadfast love" (9:17). God, if you love me, cast out my fear. All I want to do is die; give me back the psalmist's craving for life:

> Look at me, God, and rescue me—
> love me like they say you do!
> What if I die? Then I'll only forget you;
> I can't sing songs to you from the grave.
> BASED ON PSALM 6:4–5

The psalmist didn't believe in resurrection; I do. But I can't wait till heaven. Show me that eternal life starts now.

A Poem-Prayer

> Throw away thy rod
> Throw away thy wrath
> O my God
> Take the gentle path.
> FROM "DISCIPLINE" BY GEORGE HERBERT (1593–1633)

Suggestion

Memorize these lines of poetry or a phrase from Psalm 6 and repeat it to yourself during the day.

Psalm

Day and night I cry out to you
O Lord help me, save me
at night I cry myself to sleep
at sunrise I curse the light
that I face with the dawn of the day
my tears are unnumbered
they fall without ceasing
night after night my soul screams
why have you abandoned me?
why have you not heard me?
my soul is torn to tatters
my heart is pierced with grief
every moment I live I cry to you
yet still you do not answer me
can you not save my soul?
you led your people out of Egypt
you calmed the storm on Galilee
you made the lame walk, the blind see
you breathed your life into this creation
and made mankind in your image
yet you do not hear my cry
night after night I cry to you
longing for your presence again
O Lord hear my cry, listen to me
help me, heal me, save me

© SOPHIE DUTTON

Day 2

Heard

Focus: If you could make one charge against God—or against people who use God's name—what would it be? Say it to God now. God can take it.

> Get out of here, you Devil's crew:
>   at last GOD has heard my sobs.
> My requests have all been granted,
>   my prayers are answered.
> Cowards, my enemies disappear.
> Disgraced, they turn tail and run.
>
> PSALM 6:8–10 (*THE MESSAGE*)

It isn't easy to suffer from depression when you live in an apartment. I remember how I used to climb up to the unlit, concrete-walled attic space so as to scream and sob without my neighbors hearing. And once, on a holiday with other Christians, I shut myself in the bathroom with a bottle of wine and drank most of it between shouting and kicking the door.

Pride leads me to conceal my weakness and rage, but somewhere else, deep down, I long for my yells and curses to be heard—only not by the wrong person. Does God hear? Maybe, like a well-trained counselor, he is too wise to leap in with instant advice. Maybe he waits until I am ready for an answer. Sometimes I wonder if all he's saying, in between my complaints, is, "Do you want to tell me more?"

"You have . . . put my tears in your bottle. Are they not in your record?" (Psalm 56:8). Is he just listening . . . and recording? Not as a record of evidence against me, but a file of my trials, to be turned into trophies to my survival. God's records never contain inaccurate information.

If that's the case, I can confidently say to the things (and people) that oppress me: "Get out of here"—only I might choose a stronger way of putting it! Let those who look askance at me be ashamed, not me.

Reflect

"When he has tested me, I shall come out like gold."

JOB 23:10

Suggestion

If you feel up to it, try writing your own version of Psalm 6, describing your feelings. Use language as strong as you wish—no one need see it! Read it out loud to God as your prayer.

A Cry for Rescue

Save me O Lord
for the waters have come up to my neck.
I'm sinking beneath the waves Lord,
deeper and deeper every day and I don't know what to do.
I don't have the energy to swim against the tide.
I look around for a lifebelt, or some floating driftwood,
but there is nothing there.
Nothing but me and the water.
Save me O Lord
I sink deep into the mire where there is no foothold.
I have come into deep waters and the flood sweeps over me.
How did I get into this mess?
How did my life lead me here?
I am weary with crying,
and tired of trying not to cry.
How can I be strong when I feel this way?
How can I make out that I'm floating along quite happily
when the reality is so different?
O God you know my folly, my wrongs are not hidden from you.
You know why I feel this way. You know how this feels.
You know the pain that's on the inside,
even if it doesn't show on the outside.
Whilst I may feel utterly, completely alone,
you never leave my side.

Save me O Lord
for the waters have come up to my neck.
I'm sinking and I don't know what to do.
But now I know that I am not alone in the water.
There may not be a lifeboat, but there is you Lord.
At an acceptable time, O God,
in the abundance of your steadfast love,
answer me.
Don't leave me in the deep waters,
but guide me to shallow pools,
where I can once again raise my head above water
and plant my feet on solid ground.
And until that time,
be a rock that I can cling to.
The waters may come up over my head,
the flood may sweep over me,
but I can cling on to you,
knowing in time that the storm will abate
and I will have the energy to swim again.
Answer me O God
for your steadfast love is good.
Amen.

© MELISSA WILLIAMS

Day 3

Hunted

Focus: Do you see your depression as somehow your fault? Ask God to show you what the real causes are.

> GOD! God! I am running to you for dear life;
>   the chase is wild.
> If they catch me, I'm finished:
>   ripped to shreds by foes fierce as lions,
>   dragged into the forest and left
>   unlooked for, unremembered.
> GOD, if I've done what they say—
>   betrayed my friends,
>   ripped off my enemies—
> If my hands are really that dirty,
>   let them get me, walk all over me,
>   leave me flat on my face in the dirt.
> Stand up, GOD; pit your holy fury
>   against my furious enemies.
> Wake up, God. My accusers have packed
>   the courtroom; it's judgment time.
> Take your place on the bench, reach for your gavel,
>   throw out the false charges against me.
> I'm ready, confident in your verdict:
>   "Innocent."
>
> PSALM 7:1–8 (*THE MESSAGE*)

I can hear what they're saying, even behind my back. The voices echo in my head: "She's just not trying"; "She's backsliding"; "I think she just uses her depression as an excuse."

Sometimes they say it to my face:

"You're lazy."
"If you go to a professional, you're not trusting God."
"You don't need a therapist, you just need more prayer."

No one likes a depressive around them. I'm too much trouble, I demand too much. Even my nearest and dearest are getting tired of my needs and my outbursts. It must be me that's wrong, after all. I must just be too self-centered.

No, that's not right, I take it back. I didn't choose to be depressed—it's not as if I enjoy it. I'm not lazy—I do work when I can. Sometimes I just can't.

God, you know when I've really done wrong and when it's false guilt. Will you please shut up those who blame me? Or just keep them away from me? Better still, give me the courage to answer them back. I'm not a malingerer; I'm not neurotic; I'm just ill. Let them recognize I can't help it.

A Prayer

"You know all about it—the contempt, the abuse."

PSALM 10:14 (*THE MESSAGE*)

Suggestion

Write down any unhelpful things that people have said about your depression. Ask God to forgive those people. Then tear the paper up and, if you want, burn it (safely, in a container).

Day 4

Guilty as Charged?

Focus: This won't be easy, but be brave! Think of something you've done that you're really ashamed of. Say to God, "God, you know I did this and you still love me passionately." Say it as many times as you need to until you believe it.

> God, can't you stop now?
> If this is your discipline, I've had enough:
> I'm riddled with arrows from your bow,
> I sink down under your heavy hand.
> I'm shrinking to nothing because of your anger;
> my bones feel as brittle as an old person's.
> You don't have to tell me about my sins:
> they already weigh me down more than I can bear,
> I feel rotten from the inside to the out.
>
> BASED ON PSALM 38:1–5

There it goes again, that stuff about God's anger. Haven't I dealt with all that? But the trouble is, this time I think I really deserve it. This isn't false guilt. I know I've done wrong, and I can't escape from the memory of it.

What's hardest to bear is knowing that I've hurt the most important person in my life. Why are the people closest to us always the ones we hurt most? I fear I've destroyed what I value more than anything: our relationship, her trust. Why did I say those horrible things? Uncontrolled fury took over my whole body and I still feel bruised by its impact. When I'm so low, I don't seem to be able to stop the negative feelings from bursting out. The more I think about what I've done, the worse it looks. Shame adds itself to re-morse: how could I have been so stupid?

I don't feel ready to patch it up yet; I'm afraid she won't want to, or I'll say the wrong thing again. All I can do is go to God—and maybe that's the best thing to do anyway. Forgive me, Lord—I did know what I was doing. Take this burden off me, for you have al-ready borne my punishment yourself. Take the arrows of guilt and nail them to the cross; then I'll know I'm free.

A Prayer

"Lord, my longings are sitting in plain sight, my groans an old story to you. My heart's about to break; I'm a burned-out case. . . . Don't dump me, GOD; my God, don't stand me up. Hurry and help me; I want some wide-open space in my life!"

PSALM 38:9–10, 21–22 (*THE MESSAGE*)

Suggestion

Write a letter to someone you've hurt. There's no need to send it until you really feel ready to—and maybe you don't need to send it at all.

I Wake and Feel the Fell of Dark

I wake and feel the fell of dark, not day.
What hours, O what black hours we have spent
This night! what sights you, heart, saw; ways you went!
And more must, in yet longer light's delay.
With witness I speak this. But where I say
Hours I mean years, mean life. And my lament
Is cries countless, cries like dead letters sent
To dearest him that lives alas! away.
I am gall, I am heartburn. God's most deep decree
Bitter would have me taste: my taste was me;
Bones built in me, flesh filled, blood brimmed the curse.
　　Selfyeast of spirit a dull dough sours. I see
　　The lost are like this, and their scourge to be
　　As I am mine, their sweating selves; but worse.

GERARD MANLEY HOPKINS (1844–89)

Day 5

God Hurts Too

Focus: "God is without body, parts, or passions" goes a classic theological statement in the Westminster Confession. But the God of the Bible is full of emotion, often deeply hurt. What does it mean to you that God cares enough to be hurt?

> My neighbors stab me in the back.
> My competitors blacken my name,
>   devoutly they pray for my ruin.
> But I'm deaf and mute to it all. . . .
> I don't hear a word they say,
>   don't speak a word in response.
> What I do, GOD, is wait for you,
>   wait for my Lord, my God—you *will* answer!
>
> PSALM 38:11–15 (*THE MESSAGE*)

I've always found it strange the way David wrote to God in Psalm 51, "Against you, you alone, have I sinned" (v. 4). He'd seduced another man's wife, then arranged for her husband to be killed in battle. Against God alone? Maybe the answer is in the parable that Jesus, son of David, told a thousand years later. The people separated out to his left-hand side say, "Lord, when was it that we saw you hungry or thirsty or a stranger or naked or sick or in prison, and did not take care of you?" and he replies, "Just as you did not do it to one of the least of these, you did not do it to me" (Matthew 25:44–45).

It frightens me to think that when I hurt another person, even the least, by my actions or inaction, it's God I wound. But if every human being is in God's image, then it makes sense. I suppose that's why David addresses himself only to God. His business is with the only one who can forgive sins.

My spiritual reflexes aren't so refined, I fear! When I've messed up, the first thing I want to do is get back in the good graces of the person I've offended. It's what my friends think of me that I worry about. But perhaps, if I straightened matters out with God first, I might find it easier to sort them out with the other people concerned. Help me, God—I can't deal with this alone. What I need to know most is that you are still my friend.

A Prayer

Sometimes I feel like a house that hasn't had a spring cleaning for a long time. Down in the cellar, all sorts of ugly, dirty stuff is lurking. God, come in with your floodlight, your broom and mop. Shine your light on the mess I'm so ashamed of, and gently but firmly give me a good scouring out.

Suggestion

Read Hosea 11:1–4. Imagine yourself as the toddler being led by God and picked up when you fall down.

Day 6

What Does It All Mean?

F̲ocus: What's it all about? Do you sometimes ask that? I do—
and I'm sure God can cope with the question.

> I'm determined to watch steps and tongue
>> so they won't land me in trouble.
> I decided to hold my tongue
>> as long as Wicked is in the room . . .
>> But the longer I kept silence
> The worse it got—
>> my insides got hotter and hotter.
> My thoughts boiled over;
>> I spilled my guts.
> "Tell me, what's going on, GOD?
>> How long do I have to live?
>> Give me the bad news!
> You've kept me on pretty short rations;
>> my life is string too short to be saved.
> Oh! we're all puffs of air.
>> Oh! we're all shadows in a campfire.
> Oh! we're just spit in the wind.
>> We make our pile, and then we leave it . . .
> Ah, GOD, listen to my prayer, my cry—open your ears . . .
> I'm a stranger here. I don't know my way—
>> a migrant like my whole family.
> Give me a break, cut me some slack
>> before it's too late and I'm out of here."

PSALM 39:1–6, 12–13 (*THE MESSAGE*)

They say I shouldn't ask, Lord. These sort of questions aren't welcome here. They look askance at my tiny mustard seed of faith—it's not enough. My negativity is a bad witness; I should keep my mouth shut.

But I can't do it. The questions keep bursting out. What does it all mean, anyway? How long do I have to carry these feelings inside? You made me with this personality, Lord. Can I help it if it doesn't suit the party line? And I can't just ignore the troubles of the world.

I want to know the truth. Surely life isn't meant to be all happy-clappy chorus singing? Surely there's a place in your kingdom for a person like me, who sometimes gets down? Tell me, Lord—I can't be the only one. Lead me to someone who understands.

Reflect

"I know now, Lord, why you utter no answer. You are yourself the answer. Before your face questions die away."

C. S. Lewis, *Till We Have Faces: A Myth Retold* (1956)

Suggestion

Sit on the floor and imagine Jesus sitting down next to you in friendly silence. Then you begin to talk to him. What do you want to say?

Day 7

In the Desert

Focus: What upsets you most about the way you are feeling? What is the most difficult part of being depressed?

A white-tailed deer drinks
   from the creek;
I want to drink God,
   deep draughts of God.
I'm thirsty for God-alive.
I wonder, "Will I ever make it—
   arrive and drink in God's presence?"
I'm on a diet of tears—
   tears for breakfast, tears for supper.
All day long
   people knock at my door,
Pestering,
"Where is this God of yours?"
These are the things I go over and over,
   emptying out the pockets of my life.
I was always at the head of the worshiping crowd,
   right out in front,
Leading them all,
   eager to arrive and worship,
Shouting praises, singing thanksgiving—
   celebrating, all of us, God's feast!
Why are you down in the dumps, dear soul?
   Why are you crying the blues?

> Fix my eyes on God—
> soon I'll be praising again.
>
> PSALM 42:1–5 (*THE MESSAGE*)

"Why? O God, why?" I used to swear I'd never ask it. "Why me?" just begs another question: "Why not?" But now I really want to know. At least if I'd suffered a real disaster I could justify what I'm feeling, but this awful negativity comes without warning and without obvious cause. And being a Christian doesn't make it better; sometimes it makes it worse. Aren't we supposed to be full of the joy of the Lord? How can my constant misery be a good witness to my friends who don't know God?

I can barely remember the time when prayer and worship used to comfort me. Now a few scraps of your Word are all I can manage. From this "valley as dark as death" the mountaintop is only a distant memory.

"My soul is cast down within me; therefore I remember you" (Psalm 42:6). Can I summon the strength to pray? Can the memory of past celebration give me a glimpse of a possible future? "Fix my eyes on God." It's a command—to put my hope in the sheer fact of God and my relationship with him. It looks impossible now but it might just get easier with practice.

A Prayer

"I have been young, and now am old, yet I have not seen the righteous forsaken" (Psalm 37:25). Right now I don't believe it. Do just one thing to show me I'm not forsaken, Lord.

Suggestion

Try to think of just one thing you know about God—even if you don't feel too sure about it at the moment.

From Psalm 124

If the Lord had not been on our side,
then would the waters have overwhelmed us
and the torrent gone over us;
then would the raging waters have gone right over us.
Holy one, our illnesses are like the waters of the desert
There are times when they appear not to exist
and life is secure.
Then there are times when the waters come flooding through
carrying the hot loose dry sand of the desert before them
changing the familiar landscape
and sweeping us with them.
So we are never secure even when the sun is shining
and there is no sign of rain.
Be with those amongst us that are experiencing the flood.
Be with those amongst us who are fearing the next downpour
and help all of us to know that we survive
because you are with us
so that we may see the desert bloom.

© Jengie Jon

Searching for God

Dear God,
Do you exist? I think you must not,
Because surely a God would look after me.
Would he leave me unprotected and alone?
And yet, in speaking to you I am almost comforted.
Perhaps I have made you real.

© TC

Day 8

Give Me Light

Focus: Can you remember a time when the cloud of gloom lifted, even if only for a moment? Thank God for that moment; ask for another.

> Clear my name, God; stick up for me
>> against these loveless, immoral people.
> Get me out of here, away
>> from these lying degenerates.
> I counted on you, God.
>> Why did you walk out on me?
> Why am I pacing the floor, wringing my hands
>> over these outrageous people?
> Give me your lantern and compass,
>> give me a map,
> So I can find my way to the sacred mountain,
>> to the place of your presence,
> To enter the place of worship,
>> meet my exuberant God,
> Sing my thanks with a harp,
>> magnificent God, my God.
>
> PSALM 43:1–4 (*THE MESSAGE*)

Something I'd forgotten all about came back to me today. It was that moment in the empty church on vacation, all those years ago, when I suddenly felt as though I'd stepped into a force field of God's love. It was like what Jesus talks about in Luke 11:36: "Your whole body . . . full of light, with no part of it in darkness." Nothing could convince me that that experience wasn't genuine.

How far from that I feel today: my body, my soul feel full of darkness. But because I remember that piercing shaft of light, I can call on God to fill me again with his light. O how I long to be that whole, like a night watchman longing for the dawn (Psalm 130:6).

If only I could go back to that church, or to one of the special places where I've been on pilgrimage or retreat. But if God gave me that light, I wouldn't need to travel. I'd be in God's dwelling place wherever I was, because God would be dwelling in me.

"Why are you down in the dumps, dear soul?" Now I'm no longer asking the reason, but gently telling myself I don't have to stay this low. I can ask God to defend me against my enemies of frustration and disappointment; I can ask God to send light and truth, and I will be healed.

A Poem-Prayer

> How fresh, O Lord, how sweet and clean
> Are thy returns! ev'n as the flowers in spring . . .
> Grief melts away
> Like snow in May
> As if there were no such cold thing.
>
> FROM "THE FLOWER" BY GEORGE HERBERT (1593–1633)

Suggestion

Choose a short word such as "light" or "love." Sit comfortably with eyes closed, breathe deeply, and simply keep repeating the word inwardly.

A Prayer for Those Days

Jesus, I know there will be bad days
and good days for me.
On the bad days, I may not be able
to remember the good days.
On the good days, I may forget
the pain of the bad days.
Was it like that for you?
I think you too
had days of sorrow, days of joy.
You compared our lives with God
to a woman giving birth
who forgets the pain,
in the joy of a child.
But sometimes we need to remember
that each new birth will bring new pain;
that each new pain will bring new birth.
You endured the pain
because you knew joy was coming.
Teach us to believe in the joy
in the midst of the pain;
to be prepared for the pain
for the sake of the joy. Amen.

VZ

Day 9

Envy

Focus: What do you feel when you look at others who are not depressed? Do you feel that God is unfair?

> No doubt about it! God is good—
>   good to good people, good to the good-hearted.
> But I nearly missed it,
>   missed seeing his goodness.
> I was looking the other way,
>   looking up to the people
> At the top,
>   envying the wicked who have it made,
> Who have nothing to worry about,
>   not a care in the whole wide world . . .
> What's going on here? Is God out to lunch?
>   Nobody's tending the store.
> The wicked get by with everything;
>   they have it made, piling up riches.
> I've been stupid to play by the rules;
>   what has it gotten me?
> A long run of bad luck, that's what—
>   a slap in the face every time I walk out the door.
>
> PSALM 73:1–5, 11–14 (*THE MESSAGE*)

It's my besetting sin, I know—envy. Other people are always better off: they have nicer houses, better-looking husbands, less troublesome children. The non-Christians have it easy: they get the highest-paid jobs, never mind about vocation; they spend on themselves and don't give to church and charities; they stay in bed on Sunday morning; they don't wear themselves out with evening meetings.

And the other Christians have it easier too. They haven't had to cope with the struggles I have. They've been taught about God since the cradle. They feel at home in churches where I always feel a stranger. Oh yes, everyone else has it easier than me, don't they?

What have I got from serving you all these years, Lord? Wait a minute, haven't I heard something like this before? Yes, it was that sour-grapes elder son who whined about his father serving fillet steak when his wayward brother came home: "All these years I have been working like a slave for you . . . yet you have never given me even a young goat." What did the father say? "Son, you are always with me, and all that is mine is yours" (Luke 15:29, 31).

Then there were those vineyard workers who complained that the latecomers got the full daily wage. "Am I not allowed to do what I choose with what belongs to me?" said the owner. "Or are you envious because I am generous?" (Matthew 20:15).

Yes, Lord, I am envious. Lift me out of my self-pity and covetousness, and teach me to be grateful to you.

Reflect

"God is able to provide you with every blessing in abundance, so that by always having enough of everything, you may share abundantly" (2 Corinthians 9:8).

Suggestion

If you can, thank God for the gifts he has given someone else. Then you may be able to thank him for the different ones he has given you.

Broken

Lord, I asked you for a marriage
but you gave me a broken one;
I asked you for a child
but you gave me a broken one;
I asked you for a church
but you gave me a broken one;
I asked you for a life
but you gave me a broken one;
I asked you for hope
but you gave me a broken one.
Why is everything you give me
broken?
Why is every promise you give me
broken?
Is it, perhaps, that I will feel at home
with broken things
because I myself
am broken?
Or is it because you, perhaps,
are a broken God?
Perhaps that is the only God who can help me—
a broken God.

VZ

Day 10

The Story Behind

Focus: When do you feel closest to God? What makes you feel God's presence—and what difference does it make?

> If I'd have given in and talked like this,
> 　I would have betrayed your dear children.
> Still, when I tried to figure it out,
> 　all I got was a splitting headache . . .
> Until I entered the sanctuary of God.
> 　Then I saw the whole picture:
> The slippery road you've put them on,
> 　with a final crash in a ditch of delusions.
> In the blink of an eye, disaster!
> 　A blind curve in the dark, and—nightmare!
> We wake up and rub our eyes . . . Nothing.
> 　There's nothing to them. And there never was.
>
> PSALM 73:15–20 (*THE MESSAGE*)

Oh, I see it now. Somehow, when I opened up to you, Lord, I began to view life from your perspective. I saw the story behind the story. All those others, the unbelievers, who seem to be doing so well—hit them with a disaster and they'll crumble like a house built on sand. When the storms come, then we'll see who belongs to you. Not to mention the eternal outlook. What will they have to show when they come before your piercing gaze?

My own achievements aren't so hot. What is it Paul said? "Now if anyone builds on the foundation with gold, silver, precious stones, wood, hay, straw—the work of each builder will become visible

. . . because it will be revealed with fire" (1 Corinthians 3:12–13). I feel I'm more in the hay and straw business—building with scrap rather than the best bricks. But at least my problems have driven me to make sure I've got the right foundation. There's nothing like trouble to make you dig deep; and when I got to the bottom I found the Rock of Ages.

One of the stories I read over and over to my son when he was small was "The Three Little Pigs." I often wonder if it's just a folk version of Jesus' story about the houses built on sand and rock. Well, that big bad wolf comes huffing and puffing around my house pretty often, but one thing I know: what the Lord builds is solid stone, and no wolf can blow it down.

A Prayer

"When I was beleaguered and bitter, totally consumed by envy, I was . . . a dumb ox in your very presence. I'm still in your presence, but you've taken my hand. You wisely and tenderly lead me, and then you bless me."

PSALM 73:21–24 (*THE MESSAGE*)

Suggestion

If possible, go alone to a place where you have felt God's presence in the past. Just be still there for a while.

Sometimes

Sometimes the sun shines on the righteous
Sometimes the damaged tree survives
Sometimes the pain has an ending
Sometimes the darkness in us dies
Sometimes the sun shines on the righteous
Sometimes the abused forgive and grow
Sometimes there's cause for celebration
Sometimes there's meaning in the flow
Sometimes the sun shines on the righteous
Sometimes the net seems full to burst
Sometimes there's friendship in the laughter
Sometimes there's a drink for those who thirst
Sometimes the sun shines on the righteous
Sometimes God's whisper echoes far
And sometimes good's so good it beats the diamond
And shines amidst the bleakness like a star

© SIMON PARKE

Day 11

A World in Ruins

Focus: What do you feel when you turn on the television news or read the newspaper? Or can't you face doing either?

> God! Barbarians have broken into your home,
>> violated your holy temple,
>> left Jerusalem a pile of rubble!
> They've served up the corpses of your servants
>> as carrion food for birds of prey,
> Threw the bones of your holy people
>> out to the wild animals to gnaw on.
> They dumped out their blood
>> like buckets of water.
> All around Jerusalem, their bodies
>> were left to rot, unburied.
> We're nothing but a joke to our neighbors,
>> graffiti scrawled on the city walls.
> How long do we have to put up with this, GOD?
>> Do you have it in for us for good?
>> Will your smoldering rage never cool down?
>
> PSALM 79:1–5 (*THE MESSAGE*)

It's bad enough feeling useless and abandoned myself, but when I turn my eyes away for a moment to others, I don't see anything to encourage me. When I'm not suffering from envy, I'd really quite like other people to be doing better than me. It would give me hope that I too could get better.

But I look at your world, Lord, and it seems to be one disaster after another. Then I look at your church, which is supposed to be better, and it's a sorry sight. Intolerance, backbiting, indifference to the world's suffering, obsession with issues of ritual and tradition . . . it looks as though the enemy's come right inside the gates of the temple. Nonbelievers look at us and say, "What have you got to make us want to join you?" Preachers talk about healing and wholeness, but I look at my close friends and they seem to battle year after year with the same problems, even though they believe in you. Have you given up on your people, Lord?

Sometimes I get so angry and frustrated—how long can this go on? I understand now that former boyfriend of mine who used to say, "I wish it were a hundred years from now and I was in heaven."

Then I read this psalm, and I realize there's nothing new about what I'm feeling. God's people thought they had divine immunity from suffering. They couldn't understand it when pagans stormed into the heart of their holy city.

But why should God's people be exempt from the trials of life? Maybe, instead of bemoaning my fate or the failings of the church, I should do something for those who suffer more than me.

A Prayer

Father, give me the strength to be the answer to someone else's desperate prayers.

Suggestion

Take a recent newspaper and tear it into shreds. Then draw a picture of how you'd like the world to be. (It doesn't have to be great art, it's only for you.)

Day 12

For God's Sake!

Focus: If a genie granted you three wishes, what would they be?

> God, give *us* a break.
>   Your reputation is on the line.
> Pull us out of this mess, forgive us our sins—
>   do what you're famous for doing!
> Don't let the heathen get by with their sneers:
>   "Where's your God? Is he out to lunch?"
> Go public and show the godless world
>   that they can't kill your servants and get by with it. . . .
> Then we, your people, the ones you love and care for,
>   will thank you over and over and over.
> We'll tell everyone we meet
>   how wonderful you are, how praiseworthy you are!
> PSALM 79:9–10, 13 (*THE MESSAGE*)

I deserve a break—I've suffered enough. That's usually the gist of my prayers. Don't I have the right, as in the American Declaration of Independence, to "life, liberty, and the pursuit of happiness"?

No, actually I don't. I gave up all that when I was buried with Christ in baptism (see Colossians 2:12). I give it up again every year when, with my church, I repeat the Covenant Service: "I am no longer my own, but yours. Put me to what you will, rank me with whom you will; put me to doing, put me to suffering . . . let me have all things, let me have nothing." The only rights are God's. "Does the clay say to the one who fashions it, 'What are you making?'" (Isaiah 45:9).

On what basis, then, can I—can we—pray? I find a challenging answer in this psalm: it is for God's sake, not our own, that we ask for change. So often I want to say, "Look how God has blessed me. I must really be a good Christian." But what I should really say is, "Look how God has blessed me. Isn't God amazing?" And even when my prayers don't seem to be answered, I need to cry with Job, "Though he kill me, yet I will trust in him" (13:15).

I'm so ashamed when people say, "I don't think much of you Christians, you're no better than anyone else." So what? We don't claim to be better. The time to worry is when people say, "I don't think much of your God." God, make me more concerned for your reputation and less for my own.

A Prayer

"Your kingdom come. Your will be done."

MATTHEW 6:10

Suggestion

Picture yourself—or the world—as a lump of clay in the hands of a skillful, loving potter. What does it feel like? Can you trust the potter for the outcome?

Day 13

Out the Other Side

Focus: Try to remember one prayer in your life, however small, that has been answered positively.

> I love GOD because he listened to me,
> listened as I begged for mercy.
> He listened so intently
> as I laid out my case before him.
> Death stared me in the face,
> hell was hard on my heels.
> Up against it, I didn't know which way to turn;
> then I called out to GOD for help:
> "Please, God!" I cried out.
> "Save my life!"
> God is gracious—it is he who makes things right,
> our most compassionate God.
> God takes the side of the helpless;
> when I was at the end of my rope, he saved me.
>
> PSALM 116:1–6 (*THE MESSAGE*)

Isn't it strange how when you're in the dark tunnel you can hardly believe in the tiny light at the end, and yet when you emerge into the light you can hardly remember the darkness? What relief, when the gray cloud inside my head lifts—even for a moment—and lets me out into the sunshine.

It's then that I can say with true feeling, "I love the Lord," for he is indeed merciful. And what does he get from me in thanks? The promise that since my prayers are answered, I shall send some more! "I'll pray in the name of GOD" (Psalm 116:13, *The Message*).

But perhaps God really does delight in my prayers, as I delighted in my son's requests when he was small—even if, for reasons he didn't yet understand, I couldn't always meet them. ("No, John, you can't have more sweets.") Nothing moved my heart so much as that cry in the night, like when I'd forgotten to put his nightlight on. Oh the joy of taking him on my lap and comforting him. Does God love comforting me?

If you do, Lord, then I will "call on [you] as long as I live" (v. 2). Don't let me ever give up crying in the night, crying for your light; for I know that you love me and that the light will come.

A Poem-Prayer

> And now in age I bud again,
> After so many deaths I live and write;
> I once more smell the dew and rain . . .
> These are thy wonders, Lord of love,
> To make us see we are but flowers that glide:
> Which when we once can find and prove,
> Thou hast a garden for us, where to bide.
> FROM "THE FLOWER" BY GEORGE HERBERT (1593–1633)

Suggestion

Next time the sun shines, go out in it (yes, even if it's winter). Drink it in, and thank God that he sends the sun as well as the rain.

Resurrection

The saddest ambition that I have in my heart
Was sown in the black, bitter soil of shame,
Was nurtured by hands that I needed to touch.
Now it grows here and lives from every idle word
That falls from human lips, of praise and of blame:
To be someone else, to be a man worthy of love.
Yet: I know I was born to give birth to myself—
To praise you by who I am, not by who I am not—
Not to grasp after love, as if love could be held.
And, though my shame says I am flawed beyond repair
And beyond love's pale, I turn to you, my God,
In uncertain trust that you love me, crippled and bare.
Christ, you are the life in the soil of my heart,
Who will burst into flower, uniquely myself—unafraid.

© DAVID BROWER

Tree of Life

A tiny bud of hope
Barely seen on a broken tree
Which appears dead. Dark. Falling.
On a speck of green
Rustles a glimmer of hope,
A breakthrough from blackness.
All is not lost.
The fake in our midst
Might yet become real.
A tiny bud of hope has been glimpsed.

© SG

Day 14

Giving Back

F ocus: What do you look forward to doing—again or for the first time—when your depression ends? (And it will.)

> I said to myself, "Relax and rest.
> GOD has showered you with blessings.
> Soul, you've been rescued from death;
> Eye, you've been rescued from tears;
> And you, Foot, were kept from stumbling."
> I'm striding in the presence of GOD,
>   alive in the land of the living!
> I stayed faithful, though bedeviled,
>   and despite a ton of bad luck,
> Despite giving up on the human race,
>   saying, "They're all liars and cheats."
> What can I give back to GOD
>   for the blessings he's poured out on me?
> I'll lift high the cup of salvation—a toast to GOD!
>   I'll pray in the name of GOD;
> I'll complete what I promised GOD I'd do,
>   and I'll do it together with his people.
>
> PSALM 116:7–14 (*THE MESSAGE*)

I'm always amazed when I receive thank-you letters from my nieces and goddaughters for their Christmas and birthday presents. Writing those letters was such a pain when I was a child.

Am I any better at sending thank-you letters to God than I was to my uncles and aunts? It seems so paltry just to say "Thanks, Lord," but how else can I repay him for this release from darkness? "I'll lift high the cup"—that reminds me of Communion, a service I love so much. If the cup is Christ's offer of wholeness, the best way I can express gratitude is to drink deep of his love. It's so frustrating for a host when a guest just toys with and picks at the feast.

And then, there's this "complete what I promised" bit. Have I made any promises? Of course I have—the commitment I made at baptism to follow Jesus all my days. The best gift I can give God is to live the way he wants me to, not only in my private life but "together with his people"—in my work, in my play, in my prayer and worship.

All that sounds daunting when I'm still feeling so weak. But then there's "relax and rest." If God is so kind to me, dare I be any less kind to myself?

A Prayer

> O Jesus, I have promised to serve you to the end;
> be thou for ever near me, my Master and my friend . . .
> My foes are ever near me, around me and within;
> but, Jesus, draw thou nearer and shield my soul from sin.

J. E. BODE (1816–74)

Suggestion

Next time you have a chance, tell some friends of a way in which God has helped you.

❖
A Walk on the Dark Side: My Story

Nearly thirty-five years ago, in the early 1970s, in the middle of a small party in a friend's college room, I lay down on the floor and refused to move a muscle. I honestly thought I would never move again and that I would be left to die there. As it happened, within minutes a friend got me up by the creative move of tickling my feet. For the next few days, however, I was alternately withdrawn and furious, until the quiet presence of friends around me restored me to normality.

This was my first encounter with the depression that was to be my unwelcome companion for the next 35 years and is still today—perhaps will be for the rest of my life. Of course, I didn't recognize it as depression at the time: it was just a reaction to the stress of starting university life. It was also a predictable "come-down" from a perhaps unnatural "high" that I'd been on for several weeks, following a dramatic spiritual experience. It was probably aggravated by the fact that I'd fallen heavily for a fellow student, who wasn't a Christian and didn't seem all that interested in me.

I recovered, got through university life with its normal highs and lows, and enjoyed most of it. Then, in my second to last term, I returned to my college room from buying food and drink for a belated birthday party I was to have that evening to find my parents sitting on my bed looking very shaken. The worst had happened: my brother, five years older than I, had committed suicide. This was the end of nine years of mental health problems, never clearly diagnosed, and several stays in a psychiatric hospital. (I think nowadays he might have been diagnosed with generalized anxiety disorder, but they hadn't invented the term then.)

The irony was that he had recently had a spell of unusually good emotional health, much of it spent on an orthopedic ward after a bad car crash. As he got better physically, however, he deteriorated mentally and had been readmitted to a psychiatric ward just after Christmas. There, heavily sedated, he had opened a window and jumped out. The ward was on the fifth floor.

Nowadays, I probably would have been given compassionate leave from the university, and my finals would have been postponed. I suspect my parents might also have sued the hospital for putting a psychiatric ward on the fifth floor with unsecured windows. This was 1975, however, and people didn't do that sort of thing so readily. I think I had a week or so off for the funeral before getting back to work. Then I had a sort of "brainstorm," finished with my steady boyfriend in a particularly nasty way—by going off with his best friend (a relationship that was utterly disastrous)—and generally made a nuisance of myself. I was somewhat amazed, when finals came hot on the heels of all this, to come within a whisker of getting a degree with honors!

A Bad Choice

After university I needed time to recover, so I took a second gap year, in addition to the one I had taken before, and lived with my parents for a while. Then, for six months, I joined a Christian community running a conference center in the countryside—possibly the happiest time of my life.

It had been my plan to do post-graduate training in social work, but I didn't get a place on a social work course so I went for my second choice, a post-graduate Certificate in Education. I'd always had strong ideas about education, but I hated schools so it wasn't a very good choice! The main bonus of the course was that, through a personal contact, I went to live for that academic year in the local theological college, which I loved and where I made some good friends.

Once qualified, I got a teaching job in a totally new area. Although it was a "good" school, the support for newly qualified teachers was minimal. I was living alone and had only one friend in the area, a young woman I'd met in my teaching course. Teaching was definitely not for me (as I should have known), and I went steadily downhill. By the end of the first term, I was crying constantly and completely unable to go in to work.

I stayed with the parents of another friend for a week before going home yet again to my parents for an extended period of unemployment. This was the first time I was prescribed antidepressants: it was "official." I stayed on the tablets, and with my parents, for several months.

A New Direction

One of the best things that happened in that time was that I went to a vocational guidance organization where they did aptitude tests on me and declared that, with my language skills, I should definitely be working in journalism or publishing. Since I already had contacts in Christian publishing from my university days, I was advised to follow up with them. In the end, I applied for a job I'd seen advertised with a magazine publisher. On the day of my interview, my first published article appeared in the *Baptist Times* (through a contact in my church), and the editor who interviewed me was sitting reading it as I entered. I got the job!

So I moved to London—and I'm still here nearly thirty years later. The job was only as an office junior but, realizing that they had an Oxbridge English graduate on their hands, the editors soon gave me small writing and editing jobs. I absolutely loved the job and the people. It was not "good-bye" to depression, however. Even in that happy time I had bouts of "nervous exhaustion" when I would start crying uncontrollably and become unable to face any of the tasks I had to do.

One of these episodes was triggered by the house I shared in

Peckham, which was infested with cat fleas that would leap on to my legs to bite me, twenty or thirty at a time, the moment I came home from work. Again, the parents of a friend came to my rescue (my friends have some lovely parents), and I stayed with them while the house was fumigated. I later moved to an international hostel in Waterloo where I made lifelong friends and once more enjoyed the delights of community.

It was at this time that, advised by my immediate boss, I first went for psychotherapy and began to explore what might be the roots of my condition. My therapist was a Christian, which I wanted, but with some eccentricities: whenever I left, she would call down her steps as I descended them, "Have a sexy time!" (I didn't.)

Progress

Day after day I talk to a stranger
who rarely answers with words
I search the sky for signs of weather
the clouds confuse the changes
I turn to the ground and rummage
between uncounted grass blades
sometimes I catch at a small bright gleam:
a broken bead, or could it be that treasure?
I cannot afford to buy the field
day after day
but then scarce yearly to climb a hill
and chance the backward view
amazed, I gather lake, wood, mountain
whole life-size landscapes conquered
and tiny they seem from here
I take the further path with a stranger
who rarely answers with words

VZ (1980)

Ups and Downs

The next blow came when, two years into my job, I was dismissed for financial reasons. This was just at the point when my parents had decided to buy me a flat in Waterloo.

I soon bluffed my way into another job at a media magazine. During my first week there we completed purchase of my flat, and by the time I moved in the following Monday I had walked out of my job, having been treated rather like a Dickensian clerk. Strangely, years later, I met someone else who had the job after me, who was also a Christian, and she had stuck it out for only a few months!

The next few years were a round of freelance writing, short-term jobs, more freelance writing, and far too many committees. I got involved with my local parish church; joined the parish council and then became church warden; joined a locally based Christian arts organization and became a director of it; was also a director of a local Christian theater company; was in at the start of a Christian feminist organization and was soon its chair—not to mention several other bodies I briefly joined and have now forgotten. My entire social life seemed to consist of committees.

I enjoyed a lot of it and, on the work front, I got interesting opportunities, from editing youth Bible notes to being front-of-house manager for a theater.

But all this activity was interspersed with a bout of depression every eighteen months to two years. I would start with the familiar crying and "dazed" feeling, take a couple of weeks off work, take antidepressants for three months or so and, if I wasn't already in therapy, find a new therapist.

Periodically, my mother would blame the "artistic temperament" that a friend of hers had identified when I was a screaming baby (somewhat unfairly, since all babies scream sometimes). But there were many external factors that accounted for the pattern of one crisis after another. I was living alone in an interesting but stressful area (there was a noisy street market below my window where I was trying to write), I was working alone much of the time, and I was doing far too much. Some of these things I couldn't change, and others I wouldn't or didn't know how to, so I went on from crisis to crisis.

Once I even rang a friend at 1:30 in the morning and, bless her, she drove down to Waterloo from north London and took me back to her house for four days. No one else knew where I was. (My mother is still angry with me for "disappearing.")

Put a Name

Put a name to my sorrows
and I shall let them pass
loose my angry grip upon
these precious shards of glass
but the name must be grand and great
the name must be true
spoken on a hill's side
cold in the dew
o I see the name printed
printed on the page
and tears come running in a stream
releasing my rage
I let go the fragments
my palm begins to bleed
the name of my sorrows
who climbs a hill may read

VZ (1983)

Rescue

Just as I was despairing of my lonely life, along came the job from heaven. I had had a sort of "word from the Lord," while reading the Bible, that I was going to go back to a job I knew very well. I thought it might be the Bible notes editing job I had left three years earlier, but it was better than that. After a few months, I found myself walking back into a job at *Third Way*, the magazine I had worked for when I first moved to London. This job was at a higher grade than before. Not only that, but by now the magazine was edited by none other than a man I had long wanted to get to know better (for his interesting mind, I hasten to add!). The job was part-time, so I could keep up with my freelance writing, and it was just outside London, so I could happily commute the wrong way every day and get six seats on the train.

As far as the depression went, my boss was very understanding and simply said, "I employ people, not jobs, and that's part of who you are." The five years I worked there were a very special time for me and strengthened me in all sorts of ways. In fact, the year after I started, I found myself editing the magazine for most of a year while my boss was being treated for leukemia. I couldn't afford depression while that was happening.

A Proper Family

I had had several boyfriends over the years but only one relationship lasting any length of time (he was an artist—tremendous fun but completely impossible as a marriage prospect). However, I was still single, in my early thirties, and definitely not enjoying it. When was that "sexy time" going to come along?

In 1986 I went to lead seminars on feminism at a weekend run by a Christian study network that I'd only just discovered. After one of the plenary sessions, a man called Ed came up to me and declared, "I think you're fascinating."

"Oh dear,'" was my first thought. "How do I get rid of him?" Yet at the same time I had another of those "words"—a strange feeling this was going to be a very significant relationship.

At the time I was very much in love with someone else, who didn't seem to be responding. But Ed was persistent, and we became good friends. The next time I got depressed, I ran away to Cambridge, where he lived, and stayed in his room while he slept on the sofa. Ed became a major support for me and, after two and a half years, in 1988, I finally agreed to marry him.

We were married in January 1989, on my thirty-sixth birthday, and decided to buy a house in north London, near my job. Now that I was officially "settled," my parents decided to move nearer to me, so they "retired" to London from the Midlands, buying a little house just a couple of miles from us. It felt, as my Dad had said in his wedding speech, as if we were "a proper family" again. Ed also helped me learn to drive, which has been a huge improvement in my life. (Yes, I know it's not very green.)

Frustration and Crisis

Ed and I, having both been single for a long time, gave ourselves a couple of years to settle down together before our minds turned to the subject of children. I thought I was fairly neutral about whether we would have any—until we started "trying" and nothing happened. No one had told me how much women's fertility declines after the age of thirty-five, and I was now thirty-eight. Here was one more thing it seemed I couldn't have. I had waited so long for marriage, and now another door was being slammed in my face. I began to deteriorate emotionally with the sheer frustration of it.

One very good thing happened at this time. Unhappy in our Anglican church, which seemed to be getting slowly narrower in its teaching, we embarked on a program of visiting other churches in the area. I was keen to try the Mennonites, who worshipped near us, but Ed was afraid it was going to be an isolationist little sect like the one he'd grown up in (I already knew it wasn't, but couldn't convince him). On our first visit, however, we were both in tears because we felt so accepted and at home there. We became Mennonites as soon as we could and have loved being part of this tiny but influential tradition ever since.

It was soon after beginning to attend the Mennonite church that I had "the breakdown I had been promising myself for years." Perhaps now I felt as if I was in a safe place to have it! It all came to a head when Ed began to rip out our kitchen, which we were replacing. I am never very good with domestic upheaval, and when he gave me the job of breaking up the old floor with a hammer (which he thought would be therapeutic) it released something in me. I just broke down completely and began to cry and cry, without being able to stop. Ed, never having seen me in quite such a state before, phoned my parents, who came over and fetched me.

I ended up staying with my parents for about a month, in an extremely fragile state and struggling with some very frightening self-harming urges. I honestly believed that my marriage was over, that I would have to go back to living alone, being lonely, miserable, and financially dependent on my parents. I was so frightened that I couldn't be in a room on my own, and one night my parents had to sit with me until I was asleep.

None of this was helped by the fact that I had been put on a new antidepressant. The doctor had refused to put me on my usual ones, which can be dangerous in overdose—even though I have never been the least bit tempted to overdose. This new medication was doing precisely zero for my mood. I had also begun to see a classic Freudian analyst, who was about half my age and whose method (to sit and say nothing) I actively disliked. As I got a bit better, I tried to leave her to find a different type of therapist, but she just labeled this attempt as "denial"—until I took my dad, who was a retired doctor, along to support me.

Once she finally let me go, I soon found a new, Christian therapist who took a more eclectic approach. Being an art therapist, she got me to mess around with paints and clay, which was just the escape from words that I needed. I had also begun to have "dates" with Ed, and eventually moved back in with him. My life started to be put back together.

One of the bonuses of this time was the community psychiatric crisis service, which was at that time unique in the country. They sent me to a stress management course and, later, an assertiveness course, all courtesy of the National Health Service. I was also finally given an antidepressant that actually worked and had the bonus of blocking the intrusive thoughts of self-harm.

Hell

Hell is beautiful, so beautiful
but they do not give you eyes
mountains dream, and water
champs and nibbles at the rocks
but they do not give you ears
sun strokes you all day with fragrant palms
but they do not give you skin
all the dear people talk to each other
in a language you do not know
and all through hell breathes
the everywhere breath of God
but they do not give you a soul

VZ (1992)

New Life

For some time, Ed and I had been investigating the healing prayer approach called "healing the family tree," pioneered by Dr. Kenneth McAll. This involves identifying "problem deaths" in one's family tree—deaths in war or suicides who, in older times, would have been buried without ceremony in unconsecrated ground—and holding a requiem service for them, sometimes with dramatic results for the living.

After reading McAll's book *Healing the Family Tree* (Sheldon Press, 1986), Ed and I both independently came to the conclusion that we should do this for my maternal grandmother, who had died in a concentration camp. She was, in fact, my mother's adoptive mother. The biological one had been a Jewish refugee from Poland, unable to support her children, and had died in the Spanish flu epidemic of 1918–19. So it felt rather as though my infertility was inherited from my adoptive grandmother! Strangely, when I began to ask about my family tree, it turned out that my grandmother's sister and brother-in-law were also infertile, and they had perished alongside her in the camp.

After a year or so of family tree research on both sides, we had the healing service. The timing was extraordinary: having fixed the date as near as possible to my late brother's birthday, I then discovered that, two days before, there would be a weekend on healing the family tree at my favorite retreat center. Of course I attended and was duly prayed for.

Some days after the healing service, I began to feel a bit queasy. I thought it was a stomach upset—until I phoned the X-ray department where I was trying to make an appointment about an injury I'd sustained while ice-skating.

"When was your last period?" asked the appointments clerk.

"Er . . . about five weeks ago," I answered. Since my periods had become very regular over the past few years, this was definitely odd.

I lost no time in getting a pregnancy test and, on plucking up courage to use it, I found that, yes, it did turn pink. In fact, I am pretty sure I had conceived on the afternoon I returned from the healing weekend! Instantly I stopped my antidepressants, which were by then at a pretty small dose. I managed to stay off them for the crucial first three months, despite being sick all day every day for precisely three months.

At month five, however, I got depressed again. This was largely the result of reading too many books that assured me I would be "blooming" in the second trimester, and foolishly trying to write a book during that period. Thanks to the resumption of anti-depressants, and an exceptionally sunny summer during which I did nothing but eat ice cream and read books in the garden, I was blooming in my third trimester.

After a shortish but very traumatic labor, John was eventually born by forceps delivery. If we thought things were going to go smoothly from then on, we were misguided. I'd had a double epi-siotomy (cuts to help the baby out). On one side, the stitches came out and the cut became infected. I found myself back in the hospi-tal, with baby, in the gynecological ward. At one stage, all three of us were sleeping in a side ward, with Ed on a folding bed and me connected to a stationary drip fixed to my own bed, trying to feed and change John.

We finally arrived home, in great relief, but getting used to life with a demanding (and not very sleepy) baby when you're trying to recover from an infection is not the easiest task for a depressive. During my pregnancy, I had expressed the fear that I might get postnatal depression, and my psychiatrist had replied cheerfully, "You never know, you might get a manic episode." This, perhaps due to his suggestion, was exactly what I did. I grew more and more wound up until one night, wide-awake at 1:30 AM and writ-ing rather weird prayers for a thanksgiving service (which is very uncharacteristic for me—I never work at night), I realized I needed a doctor.

I was so far gone that when the duty doctor came and left a prescription marked "DR. A. LOCUM," I thought I had hallucinated him and had to ask Ed for reassurance that he'd actually been there! On a higher dose of antidepressants, I stabilized and began to get into a routine with John.

Something Wrong

We could see from the start that John was going to be an intelligent and articulate child, but not an easy one. Problems with his behavior emerged when he was at nursery, aged two and a half. In reception class at a local school, the problems escalated. By the end of two terms, he was obviously so distressed (and so was I) that I unilaterally took him out of school entirely (he was still only four) and sent him to another child minder so that I could fulfill work commitments.

There followed five very tough years. I found John a lovely Montessori school just ten minutes' drive away, where he spent three happy years. The head insisted, however, that he must have some kind of social communication disorder, so I began to apply for assessment by the local education authority.

In the meantime, there was the small matter of my finding a lump in my armpit and being told I had a rare form of breast cancer—an ectopic tumor. Fortunately it was found early, it responded well to treatment, and I am still free of it nearly seven years later; but two hospital stays for surgery and six weeks of radiation therapy obviously disrupted life considerably and didn't do much for my mental health.

My two bids for assessment for John had been unsuccessful since he was not in a local school and his academic results were up to three years ahead of his age. The day after he left the Montessori school, having grown too old for it, we saw a private psychologist. He eventually diagnosed John with NLD, or nonverbal learning disorder. (The day after that, we embarked on a three-week car tour of Europe to celebrate the end of my cancer treatment!)

We now had a diagnosis but no school. Desperate, I turned to an "alternative education" project that I had seen advertised, based a few miles from us. This was meant to be a stopgap while we fought for a statement of special needs, but John ended up staying there two years. During that time, the project moved to a location sixteen miles away from us and placed John at a Montessori school eighteen miles from us as a part-time "drop-in" pupil.

We paid someone to drive him to school but I was driving for a minimum of half an hour each way to fetch him. Not only that, but the teacher who ran the project from her home was also very keen on alternative diets and alternative medicine. Trying to keep up with her recommendations almost sent me into another breakdown! I'm very grateful for the intensive and demanding work she did with John, and he would never have been ready for school without her, but by the end we were glad to leave.

Finally, after three and a half years and three applications, we got an assessment. After another year, we had a "statement," with full-time learning support, and we were given a school place five minutes' walk from home. The school was small, kind, and set on lovely grounds, and it housed a Speech and Language unit with a vacancy in John's year, where they could work with his social communication difficulties. All my hard work had finally paid off.

More Challenges

After that year, John made the major step to a big local secondary school, five minutes' walk in the other direction. There, his problems are not over, but at the time of writing he is in a short-term residential unit where he is making tremendous progress. Years of campaigning on behalf of my son have definitely made me stronger, but not yet strong enough to come off the antidepressants I have been taking since 1992.

Meanwhile, I suffered another personal blow. My dear therapist Margaret, who had become more of a friend than a therapist and whom I had been seeing for ten years, died very suddenly of a heart attack. Extraordinarily, the person I had begun seeing as a spiritual director turned out to be not only a close friend of Margaret's but also a therapist, and I have now been seeing her for a couple of years.

Another recent development is the founding of Waving, not Drowning, the bulletin board I described in the Introduction. It's hard work at times, especially when members fall out with each other (which they do quite rarely), but it is also a tremendous support to over a hundred people, including me.

My Breed of "Black Dog"

I want to say a little about the form that depression takes for me. When I am depressed, I don't quite fit the stereotype of someone who withdraws from all social life and refuses to speak. As an "extrovert" on the Myers-Briggs personality type indicator, I am more likely to seek out company, although when I am depressed I would rather sit and watch others relating than join in with them. Depression inevitably, I believe, takes different forms with different personalities.

My pattern is almost like a mild form of bipolar disorder. I take on more and more jobs and events, getting excited about them and believing I can really handle them this time. Then suddenly I "crash," getting physical symptoms like palpitations, trembling hands, and a twitching eyelid (a useful warning sign!). I am usually ready to burst into tears at the least provocation, especially if someone is extra nice to me. I can also be more than usually irritable with my family. (I don't have the confidence to be irritable with close friends, although I might be with complete strangers, such as fellow drivers.) I can get extreme muscle tension, restless legs, or "the fidgets" in which my whole body feels as if I'd like to take my skin off.

I never get "floridly manic," however, spending money lavishly, giving it away to strangers, or talking a mile a minute. (I can talk a half mile a minute at the best of times!) Nor, since I have been on constant medication, do I get so low that I am unable to decide whether I want tea or coffee, or even whether to put the kettle on.

In early 2006, under a new psychiatrist, I took the risky step of trying a more modern antidepressant. Within days of stopping the old one, and before the new one had taken effect, I was in such a miserable and angry state that I screamed at my family, took a full jug of water off the dining table, turned it upside down and poured the water over the table, declaring, "That's how bad I feel." For the first time in my life, I actually felt suicidal and thought seriously about cutting myself. I went back on the old medication like a cat off a hot tin roof. If I have to be on it for life, so be it.

Unwanted Companions

Depression has been an unwelcome companion that has dogged my footsteps for well over thirty years, but I often think of a passage near the beginning of one of my favorite spiritual allegories, *Hind's Feet on High Places* by Hannah Hurnard. It's an old-fashioned but very wise book.

The heroine, "Much-Afraid," is about to embark on her journey from her birthplace, the Valley of Humiliation, to the High Places where the Chief Shepherd lives. The Shepherd, who pastures his flocks in her valley, has promised her two companions on the way, "two of the very best and strongest guides," carefully chosen for her. Here is an extract:

"Here are the two guides which I promised," said the Shepherd quietly. "From now on until you are over the steep and difficult places, they will be your companions and helpers." Much-Afraid looked at them fearfully. Certainly they were tall and appeared to be very strong, but why were they veiled? . . . The longer and closer she looked at them, the more she began to dread them. . . . Why did they not speak? Why give her no friendly greeting?

"Who are they?" she whispered to the Shepherd. "Will you tell me their names, and why don't they speak to me? Are they dumb?"

"No, they are not dumb," said the Shepherd very quietly, "but they speak a new language, Much-Afraid, a dialect of the mountains which you have not yet learnt. But as you travel with them, little by little, you will learn to understand their words. They are good teachers; indeed, I have few better. As for their names, I will tell you them in your own language, and later you will learn what they are called in their own tongue. "This," said he, motioning towards the first of the silent figures, "is named Sorrow. And the other is her twin sister Suffering."

Much-Afraid is, of course, terrified of going with such uncongenial companions. Yet, because she trusts the Shepherd, she takes their hands and, against all expectation, they strengthen and support her through her arduous, mysterious quest.

Some of you reading this book may know these two solemn and severe companions much more intimately than I do. I hope you know, too, that they are the choice of one who loves you and can transform you through this difficult and dark journey. As for me, looking back over my history in their company, I have been made freshly aware of how the Shepherd, though he rarely appears in person, has prepared the path for me, has lit my way or opened unexpected ways through the rocks so many times. The story of my journey with depression is also the story of a journey with God.

At the end of the book, when Much-Afraid reaches the High Places, she suddenly finds that her dour companions have been changed into two beautiful sisters, Peace and Joy; and she herself has a new name: Grace and Glory.

Dead Sea Song

The Lord is my shepherd
I shall not be in want
I am not in want but want is in me
he makes me lie down in green pastures
he leads me beside quiet waters
he takes me to the edge of frowning cliffs
he disturbs my soul
he guides me in paths of righteousness
the tall walls hem me in at each shoulder
even though I walk
even though I walk for a moment in sunlight
the clouds come down like blackout curtains
I will fear no
I fear only
goodness, without joy
I thirst
the cup brimming with salt water
will you prepare a table?
your rod and staff, menacing

VZ (2003)

A Healthy Sickness

Looking at it this way does not make depression into a blessing. It is still something we are free to fight with all the resources we can muster. But it tells us that God is present, even when we cannot feel any sense at all of that presence.

A friend of mine once told me something of which I do not know the source (perhaps he made it up himself) but which has stayed with me: "An impression without an expression leads to depression."

Later, during my breakdown, I read M. Scott Peck's book *The Road Less Traveled* (Arrow Books, 2006), in which Peck talks of "the essential healthiness of depression." I think (although I didn't take it in very well at the time) he meant that depression is a useful symptom which tells us something is emotionally wrong, just as physical pain tells us there is something physically wrong (unless we have leprosy or any other disease that destroys the pain receptors).

Perhaps my friend and Scott Peck are both saying the same thing: that depression is there to tell us of some emotional damage or disorder that needs our attention. I have often thought that I may have to keep my depression until I have heard everything it is trying to tell me. May I—and you—be a good listener.

Uphill

Does the road wind uphill all the way?
Yes, to the very end.
Will the day's journey take the whole long day?
From morn to night, my friend.

But is there for the night a resting-place?
A roof for when the slow dark hours begin.
May not the darkness hide it from my face?
You cannot miss that inn.

Shall I meet other wayfarers at night?
Those who have gone before.
Then must I knock, or call when just in sight?
They will not keep you standing at that door.

Shall I find comfort, travel-sore and weak?
Of labor you will find the sum.
Will there be beds for me and all who seek?
Yea, beds for all who come.

CHRISTINA ROSSETTI (1830–94)

❖
People in Pain: Readings About Bible Characters

Preachers, Sunday school teachers, and Christian writers often hold up Bible characters as examples or role models for us to follow. We hear of the faith of Abraham, the courage of Moses, the insight of Isaiah, and the determination of Paul. (Strangely, we hear less of the loyalty of Sarah, the courage of Ruth, the insight of Huldah, or the perception of Priscilla.)

Occasionally, the teachers remember to remind us that these were frail human people, whom God used in spite of their faults. Nevertheless, we get the impression that, overall, they were giants of faith—and this can make us feel somewhat less than adequate.

Is there anyone in the Bible who, like me at my worst times, just wants to pack it all in, who can't see any way out of despair, who wonders if there is even a God at all and, if there is, does that God care in the least about us?

Well, yes, there are dozens: men and women, young and old, rich and poor, powerful and powerless, who sink into the emotional depths, who cry out to God expecting no answer. So in this second series of readings I've selected a handful of Bible people with whom I feel I can identify. Again, they are presented roughly in the order in which they appear in the Bible.

Not all these people could be labeled as clinically depressed or having other mental illnesses. They are all, however, people in extreme emotional pain: the pain of bereavement; of loneliness; of social and financial vulnerability; of disappointment; of discouragement; or of disability. They went through feelings similar to ours, so they can help us focus on the feelings and experiences of mental distress.

Take from these readings and comments what you want and what works for you, and leave what doesn't. I've provided prayer suggestions and meditations, but there is less structure than in the first set of readings, so you may find them less demanding.

If I have put more emphasis on suffering than on healing, that is because, too often in the church, people do the opposite—trying to apply quick and easy cures to wounds that are deep and long-term. Sometimes, just having someone recognize and acknowledge the pain is the best healing you can find.

Day 15

Hagar: A Mother's Cry

So Abraham rose early in the morning, and took bread and a skin of water, and gave it to Hagar, putting it on her shoulder, along with the child, and sent her away. And she departed, and wandered about in the wilderness of Beer-sheba. When the water in the skin was gone, she cast the child under one of the bushes. Then she went and sat down opposite him a good way off, about the distance of a bowshot; for she said, "Do not let me look on the death of the child." And as she sat opposite him, she lifted up her voice and wept.

GENESIS 21:14–16

B eing a parent is a struggle at the best of times. Being a depressed parent is a double burden. Depression makes it difficult even to enjoy your children: they can seem like just one more duty you don't feel up to.

Hagar is Abraham and Sarah's servant, and Abraham has used her (there is really no other way of putting it) to try to become a father since Sarah doesn't appear to be able to conceive. But when Sarah's promised son, Isaac, comes along, Hagar and her son become a source of irritation to the proud new mother. Sarah wants all the glory to come to her and her miraculous baby, so Abraham, urged by his wife, reluctantly sends Hagar away with nothing more than a water bottle and a few well-meant words.

Perhaps you have had the experience of being sexually or physically abused. Perhaps your history is one of feeling unwanted, of not belonging. Perhaps you are a parent who doesn't feel you're coping with parenthood. Perhaps you are a lone parent, "left holding the baby." Perhaps you are mourning the end of a relationship.

Hagar's story can ring bells for people, especially women, in many different situations of abuse, loneliness, or desperation. Sometimes it is enough just to read the story of someone whose experience was something like yours, and to hear her cry.

Suggestion

Imagine you are Hagar, sitting in the desert. What does it feel like to be abandoned? To have no means of caring for your child? Let this lead you into your own cry to God.

A Liturgy for the Wounded

I bring this doll in memory of the children we were—
and also in memory of the child within us,
crying out for healing and love,
but trapped by fears and hurts.
We remember our innocence, our trust,
our complete dependence on other people,
and the times we were betrayed and abused.
Wounded healer, we offer you our hurts.
Broken mender, make us whole.
I bring sticky plasters, and all the hurts they cannot heal—
the wake-up-screaming nightmares and sleepless nights,
the fears that invade our waking moments,
the memories that rattle round our heads day after day.
We remember the search for healing, and the empty hopes,
the unanswered prayers, unfulfilled prophecies,
and wounds that all the sticky plasters in the world cannot heal.
Wounded healer, we offer you our hurts.
Broken mender, make us whole.
I bring a Barbie doll, a symbol of unattainable perfection—
and all those who struggle with their bodies and images,
the guilt, the diets, the vicious circle,
the child who looks in the mirror and weeps.
We remember those with eating disorders,
all who look at themselves with hate,
and anyone who tries to counter the lies with truth.
Wounded healer, we offer you our hurts.
Broken mender, make us whole.

I bring this candle; I acknowledge the darkness—
the long nights of solitude and despair,
the grief and tears at an unspeakable loss,
and the numbness that seeps over all we do.
We remember the isolation, the fear of the dark,
the bright neon smiles we hid behind,
the desperate prayers for hope and light.
Wounded healer, we offer you our hurts.
Broken mender, make us whole.
I bring a calendar, showing the past and the future—
our hopes, our fears, our laughs, our tears,
the memories and the dreams that haunt us,
and the hope that one day we will be free.
We remember that today is not the end,
that we have not come this far just to give up,
and our desperate hopes for the future.
Wounded healer, we offer you our hurts.
Broken mender, make us whole.
I bring the bread that is broken,
the wine that is poured out,
the prayers of all who sit here,
the fears, the hopes.
We remember the last meal,
the agony in the garden,
your fears, your hopes.
With you, we remember.

© SOPHIE DUTTON

Hagar: The Water of Life

And God heard the voice of the boy; and the angel of God called to Hagar from heaven, and said to her, "What troubles you, Hagar? Do not be afraid; for God has heard the voice of the boy where he is. Come, lift up the boy and hold him fast with your hand, for I will make a great nation of him." Then God opened her eyes, and she saw a well of water. She went, and filled the skin with water, and gave the boy a drink. God was with the boy, and he grew up; he lived in the wilderness, and became an expert with the bow. He lived in the wilderness of Paran; and his mother got a wife for him from the land of Egypt.

GENESIS 21:17–21

A favorite Bible story of mine, when I was single and lonely, was the story of Achsah, daughter of Caleb, in Joshua 15:16–19. Achsah is promised in marriage to whoever wins a certain battle. (She herself seems to have no choice in the matter.) Her cousin Othniel wins it, and so she is married to him.

The dowry her father gives, however, is less than generous: he gives her and her new husband some land in the Negev desert. Achsah urges her husband to ask her father for a field in which to grow food. It seems, however, that Othniel can't be bothered, for we next see Achsah, on her donkey, going to ask her father herself—and this is what she says: "Since you have set me in the land of the Negev, give me springs of water as well" (v. 19).

Water springs, more valuable even than a field, are the essential basis for life in a hot, dry country. As a single Christian, my life often felt like a desert, and this story inspired me to ask God for "springs of water"—people, experiences, or work that would restore me and enable me to keep going.

Hagar's story, too, involves an unexpected water spring. It is enough to fulfill her dearest wish: survival for her precious son. And "God was with the boy"—a word of hope for those of us who struggle with mental illness and parenthood.

Suggestion

Does it sometimes feel as though the desert is in you rather than that you are in the desert? Pray, "God, give me springs of water."

Answer Me

Lord
I don't want to be alone again
In this black pit of fear
The shadows gnawing at me
Stealing away my hope.
I want to reach out this time
And know you will hear
And accept what and where I am.
I don't want to be besieged in dreams
By swooping black cloaks
Which trap and enfold
This child inside.
I want to awaken and know I'm safe
Then, now and tomorrow
With no need to hide.
Please call out and say my name
Please listen and hear my fear
Please reach down and show
that you know who I am.

© CAROLINE COSTER

Day 17

Saul: Music Therapy

Now the spirit of the LORD departed from Saul, and an evil spirit from the LORD tormented him. And Saul's servants said to him, ". . . Let our lord now command the servants who attend you to look for someone who is skillful in playing the lyre; and when the evil spirit from God is upon you, he will play it, and you will feel better." . . . So Saul sent messengers to Jesse, and said, "Send me your son David who is with the sheep." . . . And David came to Saul, and entered his service. . . . And whenever the evil spirit from God came upon Saul, David took the lyre and played it with his hand, and Saul would be relieved and feel better, and the evil spirit would depart from him.

1 SAMUEL 16:14–23 (ABRIDGED)

What are we to make of this "evil spirit" tormenting Saul? Some people seek to explain away all the demon possession in the Bible by saying it was really mental illness that wasn't understood. Others try to "treat" those who are mentally unwell in their congregation by exorcism instead of sending them to a doctor. Both are mistakes.

Let's just say that, for whatever reason, King Saul had episodes of severe depression. There were no psychiatrists in those days but there was quite a lot of wisdom about human emotions. People had already observed that music, as William Congreve later put it, "hath charms to soothe a savage breast" (*The Mourning Bride*, 1697).

I find, among the people I know with depression, that some like to listen to calming music by Bach or quiet singing, while others express their feelings to a sound-track of the heaviest heavy metal rock they can find. Given the sound of the lyre, which is a kind of harp, Saul seems to have been in the first camp—and David was a skillful music therapist.

Is music, or could it be, a way of lifting your feelings when they weigh you down? What other simple measures help you to live with unhappy feelings? Mental health expert Mary Ellen Copeland suggests having a WRAP, or Wellness Recovery Action Plan—a list of actions that you know will help you. They could include seeing a good friend, going swimming, having a massage, reading a pleasant book, burning a scented candle, or having a long bubble bath—anything that helps you care for yourself.

Suggestion

Could you start writing your WRAP today? Pray that God will bring helpful ideas to your mind.

Day 18

Saul: Low Self-Image

As they were coming home, when David returned from killing the Philistine, the women came out of all the towns of Israel, singing and dancing, to meet King Saul. . . . And the women sang to one another as they made merry, "Saul has killed his thousands, and David his ten thousands." Saul was very angry, for this saying displeased him. . . . So Saul eyed David from that day on. The next day an evil spirit from God rushed upon Saul, and he raved within his house, while David was playing the lyre, as he did day by day. Saul had his spear in his hand; and Saul threw the spear, for he thought, "I will pin David to the wall." But David eluded him twice. Saul was afraid of David, because the LORD was with him but had departed from Saul.

1 SAMUEL 18:6–12 (ABRIDGED)

A Jewish story tells of a rabbi who prostrates himself before the Torah shrine and exclaims, "Lord! I am only a worm." The synagogue cantor follows his example. Finally the caretaker flings himself down and cries, "Lord! I am a mere worm." The cantor turns to the rabbi and says, "Look who thinks he's a worm now!"

It's easy, among depressed friends, to start a sort of negative contest to see who is the most worthless among us. Low self-esteem is a major component of depression, and may be either a cause or a result of it.

We wouldn't expect Saul, a monarch with total power, to suffer from low self-image. It just goes to show that emotional illness can happen to anyone, however apparently happy his or her situation. What's eating Saul here is that the popular chant after a key battle attributes ten times as much success to David as it does to him.

I suspect that this kind of "professional jealousy" is common among those in the limelight. There's always someone else whose books sell more or whose single gets higher up the charts! Comparing ourselves unfavorably with others happens in churches too.

How do we build confidence and knowledge of our own worth? Two ways might be to tell ourselves good things about ourselves and to congratulate ourselves on any achievements, however small. Congregations, too, could acquire the habit of affirming each other's gifts. Why wait until someone is dead to praise them?

Suggestion

Pray these words: God, you hate nothing that you have made. Show me that I am your beloved child.

Day 19

Jonah: Mood Swings

Then Jonah went out of the city and sat down east of the city, and made a booth for himself there. He sat under it in the shade, waiting to see what would become of the city. The LORD God appointed a bush, and made it come up over Jonah, to give shade over his head, to save him from his discomfort; so Jonah was very happy about the bush. But when dawn came up the next day, God appointed a worm that attacked the bush, so that it withered. When the sun rose, God prepared a sultry east wind, and the sun beat down on the head of Jonah so that he was faint and asked that he might die. He said, "It is better for me to die than to live."

JONAH 4:5–8

When I'm coping well, getting loads of jobs done, and generally enjoying life, my husband always gets rather worried. He knows from experience that such periods are often followed by a "crash" when I sink into the deepest depression. I don't officially have bipolar disorder ("manic depression"), but I have Internet friends who do. Perhaps the worst thing is that when you're "high," you really believe you can conquer the world and will never be down again—but then, suddenly and without warning, you are in the lowest of lows.

I think of this condition when I read the story of Jonah—on top of the world one day and suicidal the next, and all over a short-lived shrub with big leaves! Of course we know, if we have read the story, that the shrub will become a parable of how, just as Jonah values the shrub, God cares for the city of Nineveh, which Jonah is expecting God to destroy. For now, however, I'd like to treat it as an example of how, when we are emotionally vulnerable, the smallest everyday event can lift our mood or plunge us into despair.

Depression can make us very self-centered, so Jonah is more bothered about his own need for shade in the desert than about the people of Nineveh. When we are in this mood, it's hard to hold on to the fact that God cares for all our needs; it's only when we look back that we can see how we were brought through.

Suggestion

Reflect on the words of Matthew 6:8: "Your Father knows what you need before you ask him."

Day 20

Elijah: Accepting Help

Ahab told Jezebel all that Elijah had done, and how he had killed all the prophets with the sword. Then Jezebel sent a messenger to Elijah, saying, "So may the gods do to me, and more also, if I do not make your life like the life of one of them by this time tomorrow." Then he was afraid; he got up and fled for his life. . . . He . . . went a day's journey into the wilderness, and came and sat down under a solitary broom tree. He asked that he might die. . . . Then he lay down under the broom tree and fell asleep. Suddenly an angel touched him and said to him, "Get up and eat." He looked, and there at his head was a cake baked on hot stones, and a jar of water. He ate and drank, and lay down again. The angel of the LORD came a second time, touched him, and said, "Get up and eat, otherwise the journey will be too much for you." He got up, and ate and drank; then he went in the strength of that food forty days and forty nights to Horeb the mount of God.

1 KINGS 19:1–8 (ABRIDGED)

I call this "the Elijah cure": sleep, eat, sleep again, eat again, and then resume your life. I generally skip the walking for forty days and nights—although exercise is a great way of lifting your mood, if you can manage it.

Elijah's depression is a classic case of coming down with a bump after a "mountaintop" experience. After the "high" of a Christian conference, a vacation, or a career success, it can be very dispiriting to find ourselves back in the dullness of everyday life. Defeating the pagan prophets on Mount Carmel doesn't seem to have made Elijah's life any easier, but rather worse.

Into his desperation comes an angelic offer of help. Is it the food itself that makes the difference or the fact that someone cares enough to cook it for him? Few of us will have our dinner prepared by an angel but, when we are low, offers of help may come from the most unexpected people. We should not be too proud to accept them. Nor should we reject professional help when it's available.

Suggestion

Reflect on the words from "Will You Let Me Be Your Servant?" by Richard Gillard: "We are here to help each other walk the mile and bear the load."

Faith in Progress

A single glimpse;
this gleaming hope within,
silently forms in darkness
deep inside the furthest recesses of my soul;
this hint of luminescent beauty,
milk-white
clam-tight
gestating in a secret place,
nurtured in the solemn gritty dark;
this seed of faith.
This is a rough road;
limping and falling,
stumbling and crawling,
cuts and bruises,
heart-pain, blood, exhaustion,
and those tears!
Rocks
and travel dust
are in my eyes and in my ears and in my mouth.
Rare vistas of a golden city
are insufficient
to nurture hope.
But this sudden knowing,
glimpsing The Way within,
this transformation;
this is a quiet and startling gift;
these unexpected riches at my core,
this pearl of great price.

© ELIZABETH STERLING

Day 21

Naomi: Grief and Loss

So the two of them went on until they came to Bethlehem. When they came to Bethlehem, the whole town was stirred because of them; and the women said, "Is this Naomi?" She said to them, "Call me no longer Naomi, call me Mara, for the Almighty has dealt bitterly with me. I went away full, but the LORD has brought me back empty; why call me Naomi when the LORD has dealt harshly with me, and the Almighty has brought calamity upon me?"

RUTH 1:19–21

A large part of depression, for many people, is unresolved grief. Indeed, this may even be the cause of depression for some—not just bereavement but grief at the loss of a relationship; at the loss of a particular hope; or at unfulfilled dreams or lost abilities. Like phantom pain from an amputated leg, grief reminds us constantly of what is not there, of what we miss in our lives.

Naomi left her home years before with a husband and two sons, but she came back without them. She is not quite alone because her faithful daughter-in-law Ruth is standing by her, but, in the society of those days, the only way Ruth could help them survive was to scavenge the bits of grain left at the side of the field after reaping. Naomi has lost all her economic and emotional security. She feels as though she has lost her identity too. Relationships define us: "John's mom," "my boyfriend," "assistant to the editor."

Not long ago, I received a letter from a reader of *New Daylight*, who remembered my late brother at university. He wrote that he'd figured out, from what I'd written, that I was "Stephen's sister." It felt really odd to be labeled in that way because it was a part of my identity that, in one sense, ended over thirty years ago. Yet, in another sense, I am still "Stephen's sister" and always will be.

Grief casts a long shadow; but grief can diminish, and we can eventually find new relationships and new roles. Naomi did, as we will find out in the next reading.

Suggestion

Imagine that God has a "lost property office" where all lost things and people are stored. What would be in it that relates to you?

Midwinter

Endless sighing of the wind
amongst the trees that stand so barren,
bearing lifeless branches to the starless night.
Desolate and bare, the land lies
gripped in cold unyielding fingers,
held within this night that seems to have no end.
Oh my Lord what have you done?
Oh my Lord where have you gone?
Will this deep midwinter never end?
Mirages of brighter future
burn like fire on the horizon
just to turn to ashes at my faintest touch.
Hollow emptiness resounding,
echoes in a frozen landscape,
mimicking the crying of a hungry child.
Oh my Lord what have you done?
Oh my Lord where have you gone?
Will this deep midwinter never end?

© Elizabeth Sterling

Day 22

Naomi: Restoration

So Boaz took Ruth and she became his wife. When they came together, the LORD made her conceive, and she bore a son. Then the women said to Naomi, "Blessed be the LORD, who has not left you this day without next-of-kin; and may his name be renowned in Israel! He shall be to you a restorer of life and a nourisher of your old age; for your daughter-in-law who loves you, who is more to you than seven sons, has borne him." Then Naomi took the child and laid him in her bosom, and became his nurse. The women of the neighborhood gave him a name, saying, "A son has been born to Naomi." They named him Obed; he became the father of Jesse, the father of David.

RUTH 4:13–17

Some years ago, when I was researching my ancestry, I was struck by how my immediate family just petered out at my generation. Neither my uncle nor my aunt had children; nor did my mother's uncle and aunt; nor did my brother who died at 27, unmarried. If my part of the family was to go on at all, it was down to me, and I was having difficulty conceiving. You can imagine what a joy it was, to me and my husband and to my parents, when my son was born.

I can understand, therefore, Naomi's joy at becoming a "grand-mother-in-law." When life seemed to be over, suddenly there was new life for her, a new identity, and a new role. Of course, child-birth is not the only way of being involved in new life. There can be all kinds of restoration in our lives: a new relationship, a new career, the discovery of gifts we didn't know we had, or a hobby that gives us satisfaction and a sense of worth.

What, for you, has been or could be a "restorer of life"? What makes you feel connected to life? What makes you feel that you are a valuable person? Can you give it a bigger place in your life?

Suggestion

Reflect on God's promise in Revelation 21:3–4: "God himself will be with them; he will wipe every tear from their eyes. Death will be no more; mourning and crying and pain will be no more."

Day 23

Ecclesiastes: Disillusionment

Vanity of vanities, says the Teacher, vanity of vanities! All is vanity. What do people gain from all the toil at which they toil under the sun? A generation goes, and a generation comes, but the earth remains forever. The sun rises and the sun goes down, and hurries to the place where it rises. The wind blows to the south, and goes around to the north; round and round goes the wind, and on its circuits the wind returns. . . . All things are wearisome; more than one can express; the eye is not satisfied with seeing, or the ear filled with hearing. What has been is what will be, and what has been done is what will be done; there is nothing new under the sun.

ECCLESIASTES 1:2–6, 8–9

Maybe it's because I'm now middle-aged that I think of Ecclesiastes as a book written by someone who's middle-aged or older. Surely such cynicism couldn't come from a young person. But it can—anyone who finds life difficult can reach a point where nothing seems worthwhile, where all human life seems pointless and meaningless.

As usual, Shakespeare gets it right:

> Life's but a walking shadow, a poor player,
> That struts and frets his hour upon the stage,
> And then is heard no more; it is a tale
> Told by an idiot, full of sound and fury,
> Signifying nothing.
>
> (*MACBETH*, ACT 5, SCENE V)

Ecclesiastes' answer is simple: enjoy yourself while you can (2:24). But what if you can't? Some faiths hold out the promise of escape from the cycle of birth and death into nonexistence. The Bible as a whole sees it differently: life is not an endless vicious circle but a journey with a goal—"the renewal of all things" (Matthew 19:28). We wait for a new world, where God's love rules.

Of course, we have been waiting a long time, and even the early Christians got impatient, wondering when this great restoration would come: "We walk by faith, not by sight" (2 Corinthians 5:7). Sometimes, like Ecclesiastes, we will not even feel that faith. This is the time to rely on the faith of others whom we trust. Who can "carry" faith for you?

Suggestion

Reflect on the words from Romans 8:20–21: "The creation was subjected to futility . . . in hope that the creation itself will be set free from its bondage to decay and will obtain the freedom of the glory of the children of God."

Day 24

Job: Why Was I Born?

After this Job opened his mouth and cursed the day of his birth. Job said: "Let the day perish in which I was born, and the night that said, 'A man-child is conceived.' Let that day be darkness! May God above not seek it, or light shine on it. Let gloom and deep darkness claim it. Let clouds settle upon it; let the blackness of the day terrify it. That night—let thick darkness seize it! let it not rejoice among the days of the year; let it not come into the number of the months. Yes, let that night be barren; let no joyful cry be heard in it. . . . Let the stars of its dawn be dark; let it hope for light, but have none; may it not see the eyelids of the morning—because it did not shut the doors of my mother's womb, and hide trouble from my eyes."

JOB 3:1–7, 9–10

One thing I've noticed among depressed people is that birthdays, which should be a reason for celebration, are often disliked. Perhaps it's because birthdays bring us together with family members whose company we may not enjoy, or because they remind us that we are getting older and haven't achieved what we think we "should" have done by that age.

I don't know if birthdays were celebrated in Old Testament times, but Job, suffering multiple bereavements, having lost almost everything and everyone that mattered to him, sees the day he was born as a day that should never have happened. To wish we had never been born is perhaps the worst feeling we can have. Only the truly desperate think in this way.

The trouble is, when we are really low, all we can remember are the disappointments, hurts, and mistakes of our life. The good memories might as well not exist, because we can't believe in them anymore and they don't seem enough to balance out the bad. Our whole life feels like a mistake.

Easy answers such as "God doesn't make junk" are no real help because they don't reach down into the deep sadness and self-hatred. The best we can do at such moments is to hang on to the knowledge that these times pass—because they do.

Suggestion

"You knit me together in my mother's womb" (Psalm 139:13). Ask God to help you believe it.

Why?

So, Lord, tell me why you planned this?
I would like to know.
You made me, and have your hand on me,
but where are you?
In the dark times of pain, you feel so close
yet so far away.
So, Lord, tell me why you planned this?
I would like to know.
I feel I have no words to say, but my
fingers keep typing away
trying to find some reasoning,
trying to work out why,
so Lord tell me!
Why did you plan all this?
I would like to know.
You made the sun, the stars and the sea.
You made this world,
this life I live
which sometimes wonders where you are.
So, Lord, tell me why you planned this?
I would like to know.
Sometimes I can't see clearly through the thick black cloud
but sometimes I look out and see light.
I cry out to you, God, time and time again,
asking, searching, needing, wanting. . . .
So, Lord, tell me why you planned this?
I would like to know.

© HELEN

Day 25

Lamentations: Blaming God

I am one who has seen affliction under the rod of God's wrath; he has driven and brought me into darkness without any light; against me alone he turns his hand, again and again, all day long. . . . He has besieged and enveloped me with bitterness and tribulation; he has made me sit in darkness like the dead of long ago. He has walled me about so that I cannot escape; he has put heavy chains on me; though I call and cry for help, he shuts out my prayer; he has blocked my ways with hewn stones, he has made my paths crooked. . . . He has filled me with bitterness, he has sated me with wormwood. He has made my teeth grind on gravel, and made me cower in ashes; my soul is bereft of peace; I have forgotten what happiness is; so I say, "Gone is my glory, and all that I had hoped for from the LORD."

LAMENTATIONS 3:1–18 (ABRIDGED)

I have forgotten what happiness is.

What a heart-rending statement! Yet it's common among people suffering depression or other mental illnesses. The shadow casts itself over past, present, and future, so that we can't remember what it felt like to be well.

Why? Who's responsible? We may blame our parents, who (to paraphrase poet Philip Larkin) "messed us up." But, as Larkin points out in one of his poems, they were messed up in turn by their parents, and their parents by their parents, and so on, presumably back to Adam and Eve—which just shows how insightful the Bible is about the human condition.

If not our parents, then what about other people who have abused or rejected us? The author of Lamentations could blame the Assyrian empire that had conquered Jerusalem, or the Israelites who were not listening to his prophecies. Indeed, there may be people who have contributed to our illness, but they'll never admit it, so cursing them gets us nowhere (although, of course, if someone has actually committed a crime against us, they should be prosecuted).

Perhaps it's safer, then, to blame God, who ultimately is responsible for everything that happens in the world. Why, though, does he allow such suffering? It's a mystery. All I can say is that God doesn't mind taking the blame. It's exactly what Jesus did on the cross.

Suggestion

Speak your mind to God about your illness. God can take it.

God's Answer

I never promised to give you an easy life.
Never said you would be safe,
never promised you would be free from the cares
and trials of this world.
I never promised you wouldn't stand alone in a crowd,
or swear at the sky in frustration,
I never said you wouldn't kneel at the altar in grief and tears.
I said you would have life.
Life with all its cares, with its pain and fear and grief.
Life with its moments when you just can't find a way to go on.
Life with the sacrifices you make just to watch your work crumble
around you.
Life when a single moment of peace seems to make all the fear and
worry worthwhile.
Life in all its fullness.
I promised I would always be with you,
not that it would be easy, not that you would never feel alone.
I promised you strength no matter how weak you feel,
hope of hope as well as your despair.
I promised you life.
Life with all the beauty in the nature surrounding you,
the crashing of the stormy waves, the warm summer sun.
Life with all the connections, in community,
in friends, in families.
Life with its sudden laughter that rings in your ears
for days and days.
Life in all its fullness.

© Sophie Dutton

Day 26

Antiochus: Disappointment and Frustration

King Antiochus was going through the upper provinces when he heard that Elymais in Persia was a city famed for its wealth in silver and gold. . . . So he came and tried to take the city and plunder it, but he could not because his plan had become known to the citizens and they withstood him in battle. So he fled and in great disappointment left there to return to Babylon. Then someone came to him in Persia and reported that the armies that had gone into the land of Judah had been routed . . . that the Jews had grown strong . . . that they had torn down the abomination that he had erected on the altar in Jerusalem; and that they had surrounded the sanctuary with high walls as before, and also Beth-zur, his town. When the king heard this news, he was astounded and badly shaken. He took to his bed and became sick from disappointment, because things had not turned out for him as he had planned.

1 Maccabees 6:1–8 (abridged)

This reading is from the Apocrypha, accepted as "deuterocanonical" scripture by the Catholic Church but not by Protestants (or Jews). I include it, not as Scripture, but partly because it makes me laugh (mainly at myself) and partly because it paints such a vivid picture of how we react when life doesn't go our way.

Antiochus was a brutal dictator, yet I feel almost sorry for him. I, too, often feel sick from disappointment, because life has not worked out the way I planned. When it all gets too much for me, I take to my bed and try to escape from it all in sleep.

We can feel disappointed for our future as well as our past, knowing that it may be too late for the career we wanted or that we are unlikely to find a marriage partner or that we will never have children. As the previous reading put it, "Gone is my glory, and all that I had hoped for from the LORD" (Lamentations 3:18).

Can we overcome such disappointment? Antiochus couldn't, but the writer of Lamentations thinks we can: "This I call to mind, and therefore I have hope: The steadfast love of the LORD never ceases, his mercies never come to an end; they are new every morning; great is your faithfulness" (3:21–23).

Suggestion

If you cannot yet say, "Great is your faithfulness," pray that you will one day be able to say it.

A Day in Bed

Lord, today has been and it has gone.
I believe your sun rose and set,
that your creatures awoke
and went about their business
before heading back to bed.
I believe there has been
joy and grief
birth and death
love and war
but none of this have I seen.
Rather today has been for me
the darkness of a sleeping mind
the warmth of bed clothes
and the silence of thick walls.
It is as if today has not been.
What can I praise you for
when nothing has happened?
What can I say sorry for
when I have done nothing?
And who can I pray for
when I have not been aware
of their needs?
So like today my prayer
is full of nothing.

© JENGIE JON

Day 27

"Legion": Torn Apart Inside

They came to the other side of the sea, to the country of the Gerasenes. And when [Jesus] had stepped out of the boat, immediately a man out of the tombs with an unclean spirit met him. He lived among the tombs; and no one could restrain him any more, even with a chain. . . . Night and day among the tombs and on the mountains he was always howling and bruising himself with stones. . . . Then Jesus asked him, "What is your name?" He replied, "My name is Legion; for we are many." . . . Now there on the hillside a great herd of swine was feeding; and the unclean spirits begged him, "Send us into the swine; let us enter them." So he gave them permission. . . . Then people came to see what it was that had happened. They came to Jesus and saw the demoniac sitting there, clothed and in his right mind, the very man who had had the legion; and they were afraid.

MARK 5:1–15 (ABRIDGED)

Nowadays we might find a diagnostic label for this poor man, multiple personality disorder perhaps. But maybe it doesn't matter what he "had," just that he was living worse than an animal. He was an outcast from society and everyone feared him.

Before healing him, Jesus asks him, in effect, "Who (or what) are you?" Note that Jesus is not asking the man this question; he is asking the demon(s) or illness. Diagnosis is not always possible or even helpful, but sometimes the first step in our healing is just to name our affliction. To know that we have an illness, and are not lazy, selfish, or obstinate can be a huge relief.

What about the mass porcine suicide when the demon-possessed pigs plunged off a cliff and drowned? To me, this says that the man's problems have a life of their own and are not caused by his sin or weakness. "Sending" them into the pigs is a powerful way of sym-bolically driving them away. Some forms of therapy include ways of "acting out" our illness: speaking to it or to a chair representing a key figure in our life.

I love that ending: "clothed and in his right mind" (v. 15). Clothes are among the things that define us as human. Often, being able to dress in the morning and not lie around in pajamas all day is the first sign of getting better.

Suggestion

Dress up nicely today, even if you're only going for a walk or on an errand.

Day 28

How Long, O Lord?

Now in Jerusalem by the Sheep Gate there is a pool, called in Hebrew Beth-zatha, which has five porticoes. In these lay many invalids—blind, lame, and paralyzed. One man was there who had been ill for thirty-eight years. When Jesus saw him lying there and knew that he had been there a long time, he said to him, "Do you want to be made well?" The sick man answered him, "Sir, I have no one to put me into the pool when the water is stirred up; and while I am making my way, someone else steps down ahead of me." Jesus said to him, "Stand up, take your mat and walk." At once the man was made well, and he took up his mat and began to walk.

JOHN 5:2–9

What a strange question: "Do you want to be made well?" What else was he doing by the famous healing pool?

We all want to be well, don't we? I'm not so sure. Sometimes, especially if depression has gripped us for a long time, the idea of being without it is quite frightening. What might people (or God) expect of us if we suddenly weren't depressed?

Actually, I think this man at the pool was depressed. Perhaps, at first, it was his limited mobility that stopped him from getting into the pool, but after thirty-eight years "I can't get in" must have become a litany that he repeated without even thinking about it. Perhaps he had just got used to being helpless and didn't recognize help when it came.

It can indeed seem, as it did for this man, that every time we are "making our way," someone or something knocks us back again. I felt like that earlier this year when, while I was coping very badly with a medication change, a man snatched my handbag in a supermarket parking lot. Why was God letting this happen when I was already so emotionally weak?

Yet somehow, we progress in our own halting way, two steps forward and one step back, and often it seems the other way around. Still, I believe that Jesus can cut through our discouragement, the repeated blows that life dishes out; and, amazingly, whether slowly or quickly, early or late, he can transform our lives.

Suggestion

Pray these words: Jesus, help me to cope when things appear to go backward, and take me that extra step forward.

Say "Yes"

Loving God, we bring to you those
who were wounded before they had strength
or courage to say "No;"
who were wounded by those
who were meant to love them,
who were wounded by the carelessness of life.
We bring to you those
who when they tried
to display their wounds to others
received the answer, "No;"
who were ignored, or dismissed with a text,
who were told they lacked faith.
We bring to you those
who have been wounded a long time,
who are afraid they will never be whole.
Loving God, you still have the scars
of the wounds we gave you;
when the wounded come to you in despair,
will you welcome them?
Please, oh please, God, say
"Yes."

VZ

❖
Don't Give Me Proverbs!
An Exploration of Depression and Faith

"Rejoice in the Lord always; again I will say, rejoice."
"Do not worry about tomorrow. . . ."
"A glad heart makes a cheerful countenance."

Ever had verses such as these from Philippians, Matthew, and Proverbs quoted to you? Has anyone ever said to you, "Cheer up, it may never happen"? When anyone says this to me, I feel tempted to reply, "That's what I'm depressed about!" There is never a shortage of people who think depression and sadness can be cured by words. Don't they know that, if we thought it was true, we would have said those words to ourselves already?

False Friends

When it comes to depression and Christian faith, things get more complicated. Many churches like to feed themselves solely on the more upbeat bits of Scripture and sing only the most gung-ho of worship songs. They have no conception of how it feels to be made to sing "I will sing of your love forever" or "All of my days, I will give praise" when you feel like bursting into tears at every moment, and you're not even sure there is a God, let alone whether God loves you.

Others will tell you, "Christians shouldn't be depressed" or "You haven't enough faith." Would they say, "Christians shouldn't get a cold" or "Christians shouldn't break their wrists"? Perhaps a few would! "Health and wealth" or "prosperity gospel" churches are springing up everywhere, and there is little place for the depressed in them. There are even schools of Christian counseling that claim to heal depression by the application of carefully selected Bible verses.

132

Such false friends are likely to load us with yet more burdens rather than helping us bear the ones we already have, yet it is hard to resist their voices. The trouble is that depression or other emotional illnesses hit us in just the same place where our faith seems to reside. It is very possible to feel cheerful and sing praise songs when you are laid up with a broken leg. It is a lot harder to do so when it is your feelings themselves, through which you experience your faith, that are damaged.

Depression or mental illness can seem to strike at the very roots of who we are. How can we have "the peace of God, which passes understanding" when our hearts are torn apart with grief, anxiety, self-hatred, and anger? How can we believe that an invisible God loves us when we don't even believe that our closest friends really love us?

If our understanding of faith is that it is supposed to make us feel good at all times, then when the good feelings go away, so does the faith. This is not "backsliding" or "wandering from the way." It is illness, which we can neither prevent nor shake off.

Faith, Not Feelings?

The evangelical circles in which I spent my youth used to place a lot of emphasis on "faith, not feelings"—that is, the fact that God is real whether or not we feel God's presence. Thankfully, this spiritualization of the "stiff upper lip" is less fashionable since the charismatic movement. Like most partly true statements, however, it does have some value. In some places, the Christian faith has now gone to the opposite extreme, where our faith is totally dependent on the number and intensity of overwhelming spiritual experiences that we can muster. Feelings are all.

Perhaps we need to look at what faith really is. I don't think that faith, as the word is used in the Bible, is a matter of gritting our teeth and, like the Red Queen in Lewis Carroll's *Through the*

Looking Glass, believing "six impossible things before breakfast." Nor is it necessarily acting as though we believe, even when we don't. (There may be a place for this, especially when it comes to how we treat other people: we can still try to act lovingly toward others even when we are at our lowest ebb.)

I think, however, that "faith" in the sense that the Bible uses the word is more like a mixture of trust and commitment. I have a very reliable husband whom I trust with everything major, even if I don't always show it (I find it hard sometimes to trust him to get the right food from the supermarket!). At times, like every married person, I get thoroughly annoyed with him. At times, I follow him around, trying to make sure he does things "the proper way." (I still haven't managed to teach him to fold laundry the way I do!) Yet, if it came to a real crisis, I know I could always trust him to do whatever he thought best for my welfare.

My trust of Ed is based on past experience and knowledge of what sort of person he is and how he cares about me. Is it the same with God? Many Bible teachers tell us to trust God on the basis of God's promises in the Bible. This may work for some, but I've never found it that helpful. It seems a bit like trusting that an electrical appliance won't break down because it came with a guarantee. Trusting on the basis of a promise about the future is pretty difficult unless we have some past experience of the company and know that they are trustworthy.

Such trust is especially difficult for those whose parents or family have not been trustworthy and who have perhaps never encountered another person in their life whom they could fully trust. It is all very well for others to say, "Trust in God," but what does that mean to someone who has never experienced real trust?

To continue with our appliance analogy, we might trust the brand we buy because others whom we know or have heard of have had a good experience with that brand. Perhaps we believe the "testimonies of ordinary customers" quoted on their advertisements, or perhaps our friend has this brand of appliance and has never had any trouble with it.

Similarly, we might have faith in God because we have seen what a difference Christian faith has made to someone else's life. Yet, for a depressed person, even this route to faith is more difficult. A major component of depression, for many, is a feeling that we are the worst and most unworthy person in the world. Christian faith, marriage, or a particular approach to mental health might work for others, but it can't work for me because I am not good enough to be loved by God, a partner, or a therapist. I am the lowest of the low, and that is where I ought to stay.

In all these ways, depression makes faith ten times harder for a depressed person than it is for anyone who has never experienced depression.

Cruel and Unusual

Therefore, to say to such a person, "Just have faith" is a peculiar form of mental and spiritual cruelty. To say, "If you had more faith, you wouldn't have got depressed" is even worse. A person with depression can't muster faith as defined by this sort of remark, and Christians get depression just as Christians get flu or repetitive motion injury, because depression is an illness, not an attack from the Devil.

It's very easy to refute from the Bible the idea that the person of faith will always have an easy life and will never encounter any suffering. You have only to read the Psalms or the book of Job or, indeed, the story of Jesus' own life or the story of his first followers. Suffering is an intrinsic part of life, and we would hardly expect God to exempt those who follow him from it. (What would you think of a God who allowed only the Christians to survive an earthquake, for example?)

Christians will encounter the everyday obstacles, griefs, and losses of life just like anyone else. Some will also suffer persecution directly because of their faith. The difference, perhaps, for us is that we see our suffering as having a purpose and even a redemptive value: "Beloved, do not be surprised at the fiery ordeal that is taking place among you. . . . But rejoice insofar as you are sharing Christ's sufferings, so that you may also be glad and shout for joy when his glory is revealed" (1 Peter 4:12–13). It's as though we, like Jesus, have to go through suffering in order to experience resurrection joy. Of course, at the time we are experiencing the suffering, it is not easy to catch a glimpse of the joy ahead, or even believe in it.

Keeping the Faith

What if you are a Christian and you have depression—and you don't want to lose your faith because of it?

I think there are a number of practical things we can do to sustain some sort of faith in the midst of the "Slough of Despond" (as John Bunyan in *The Pilgrim's Progress* described depression).

First, avoid any church where people peddle easy solutions for depression, especially if these false cures are marketed as biblical. As a song by the late and recently rediscovered British singer/songwriter Nick Drake puts it, "there's really no way of ending your troubles with things you can say" (from "Time Has Told Me" by Nick Drake).

Try to find a church where depression is accepted and seen as an illness and where a depressed person is not seen as an outcast or a freeloader—at least, there should be one or two people in the church who tell it like it is.

If you can't find a church like this and your own church just makes you feel worse, then don't go to church for a while. Use an online devotional site like RBC Ministries (www.rbc.org) or All About Prayer (www.allaboutprayer.org). There is really no point in going to church just to be made to feel your faith is inadequate. Maybe, when you're better, the church will have changed or you will find somewhere more accepting.

Second, ignore all voices that say, "You don't need medical care, you just need prayer for healing." I bet they wouldn't say that if you had an E-coli infection or pneumonia! Get to the doctor, take medication if it's recommended, and find a therapist. The amount of your faith is not measured by how little you use help based on medical science.

Third, examine your image of God and from where you got it. A Christian therapist (if you can get one) or a spiritual director, or even some wise spiritual reading (*Disappointment with God* by Philip Yancey) can be of help here. Is your God a big ogre whose main occupation is waiting to catch you in a sin or a distant God who isn't really interested in the details of your daily life? Or is he even a male, stiff-upper-lip God who is a little embarrassed when women (or men) show too much emotion?

If your image of God is a damaging one, where can you find and foster a better image? The Bible is a possibility, since there are countless places in it where God is portrayed in more compassionate and sensitive terms—but you have to learn to read the Bible for yourself and not through others' spectacles. Finding Christian people who seem to know the true loving God can also help. However, before you can internalize the belief that (in Adrian Plass's words) "God is nice and he likes us," you may need to yell some very rude words at the false, angry, or nitpicking "god" you have been carrying about with you. The real God won't mind this at all since that nasty god is an idol, and the Bible is full of rudeness to idols.

Another reason the Bible can be of help (as I hope you've seen from the Bible readings in this book) is that it contains innumerable instances of people despairing, losing sight of God, crying out in pain—in fact, feeling just like we do when we are depressed.

If you get to know them, you will probably also find a number of people around you who are struggling, or have struggled, with emotional problems. Try to find the ones who don't say, "But since I became a Christian it's all been wonderful!" Those who do are the ones to avoid.

By Your Fingernails

If all this sounds like a simple prescription for an easy way to hang on to God, I don't mean it that way. Going through depression, especially if it's severe and long-term, is like going through hell, and in hell it's extremely difficult, if not impossible, to believe in God. Sometimes we will feel as if we are merely hanging on to God by our fingernails; sometimes as if we've already let go and are plummeting down the cliff into the darkness of the abyss.

When it's like this, the most important thing to tell ourselves, over and over again, is that it is not our fault. It is not because we are bad people or have failed to practice spiritual disciplines that we are depressed or suffering from doubts. Depression is an illness, and because it is one that attacks the core of our personality, it also attacks the core of our faith.

There may be times when we have to cry not only "I believe; help my unbelief" (Mark 9:24), but also "Lord, I don't believe; help me to believe." There may be times when we have to let the faith of others carry us, like the paralyzed man whose friends lowered him through the roof to see Jesus (2:3–4). The relationship of faith and mental health is a complex and varying one, and there are no easy answers. The best you can say is that faith and depression are not mutually exclusive. They can coexist and, for some people, they have to.

Jesus said to Thomas, "Blessed are those who have not seen and yet have come to believe" (John 20:29). I think he was speaking not only about believers who came later and would not have seen him in the flesh. I think he also meant those for whom the journey of faith appears to be a journey totally in the dark, without ever seeing any miracles or any seeming harvest, or even more than a glimpse of the destination. Blessed are you when you are afraid, lonely, discouraged, despairing, bitter, cynical, self-hating—and yet believe. That shows true strength and courage.

Jesus also said, "Blessed are those who mourn, for they will be comforted" (Matthew 5:4). In spite of everything, I choose to hold on to that hope.

A Vision

One day I will wake up
and the sky inside me
will not be grey.
One day I will wake up
without the pit of fear
my stomach plummets into.
One day my hands will not shake,
my legs not tremble.
One day there will be no tears
except healing tears.
One day the news won't all be bad.
One day I will look in the mirror
and smile.
One day I will want to stroke my skin
instead of cutting it.
One day food will be my friend
and not my enemy.
One day I will master drink
and it won't master me.

One day I will believe.

I am worth the same
as any other person.
One day I will be able
to receive and give love.
One day I will work
and enjoy my work.
One day I will play
and really play.
One day no one will use words like
nutjob, headcase, or jerk.
One day no one will say,
"Christians shouldn't be depressed"
or "Just have more faith."
One day churches will be
places to be your real self in.
One day I will pray and sing
and mean it.
One day I will know who I am.
One day I will love who I am.
One day.

VZ

Resources

The following resources may be of help and are included here as a guide to finding the services and programs that are a good fit for an individual's particular needs. The publisher is not recommending any specific program or service. Please consult your doctor, pastor, or licensed counselor concerning appropriate medical and counseling services.

The Christian Care Network (CCN) is a national referral network of state licensed and/or certified professional counselors offering care that is distinctively Christian and clinically excellent. Each member of the CCN has attested to being a current member in good standing with the American Association of Christian Counselors, having current state license and/or certification, and having appropriate and adequate professional liability insurance. To find a counselor, go to the American Association of Christian Counselors Web site (www.aacc.net) and click "Find a Counselor."

The site www.christianadvice.net offers Bible study guides, references, and advice on many different topics and information on the best Christian Web sites, stores, books, counselors, helps, and resources. See especially "Depression Help" at www.christianadvice .net/christian_depression_help_advice.htm.

The site www.depression.com offers information designed to help you get the facts and learn how to manage depression. (Note: this Web site is funded and developed by GlaxoSmithKline Pharmaceuticals.)

The site www.about.com/health provides basic information and links on bipolar disorder, borderline personality disorder, autistic spectrum conditions, and other mental health issues.

Books

Sue Atkinson, *Building Self-Esteem: A Practical Guide to Growing in Confidence* (Lion Hudson, 2001).

Sue Atkinson, *Climbing Out of Depression* (Lion Hudson, 2005).

Sue Atkinson, *Pathways Through Depression* (Lion Hudson, 2004).

Steve and Robyn Bloem, *Broken Minds: Hope for Healing When You Feel Like You're Losing It* (Kregel, 2005).

Les Carter, *The Freedom from Depression Workbook* (Thomas Nelson, 1996).

C. S. Lewis, *A Grief Observed* (Faber, 1966).

Pamela Rosewell Moore, *Finding Your Way Through Depression* (Baker, 2005).

David Seamands, *Healing for Damaged Emotions* (David C. Cook, 1991).

Granger E. Westberg, *Good Grief* (Augsburg Fortress, 1986).

Philip Yancey, *Disappointment with God* (Zondervan, 1997).

Philip Yancey, *Where Is God When It Hurts?* (Zondervan, 1997).